The Gild of St. Mary, Lichfield

Early English Text Society.

Extra Series, No. CXIV.

1920 (for 1914).

NEW YORK: C. SCRIBNER & CO., LEYPOLDT & HOLT
PHILADELPHIA: J. B. LIPPINCOTT CO.

The Gild of St. Mary, Lichfield

Being Ordinances of the Gild
of St. Mary, and other documents

EDITED BY THE LATE
DR. F. J. FURNIVALL

LONDON:
PUBLISHED FOR THE EARLY ENGLISH TEXT SOCIETY
By KEGAN PAUL, TRENCH, TRÜBNER & CO., Ltd.,
BROADWAY HOUSE, LUDGATE HILL, E.C.
AND BY HUMPHREY MILFORD, OXFORD UNIVERSITY PRESS,
AMEN CORNER, E.C., AND IN NEW YORK.

OXFORD
UNIVERSITY PRESS

Great Clarendon Street, Oxford OX2 6DP
United Kingdom

Oxford University Press is a department of the University of Oxford.
It furthers the University's objective of excellence in research, scholarship,
and education by publishing worldwide. Oxford is a registered trade mark of
Oxford University Press in the UK and in certain other countries

© The Early English Text Society 1920 (for 1914)

The moral rights of the authors have been asserted

Database right Oxford University Press (maker)

First Edition published in 1920 (for 1914)

All rights reserved. No part of this publication may be reproduced,
stored in a retrieval system, or transmitted, in any form or by any means,
without the prior permission in writing of Oxford University Press,
or as expressly permitted by law, or under terms agreed with the appropriate
reprographics rights organization. Enquiries concerning reproduction
outside the scope of the above should be sent to the Rights Department,
Oxford University Press, at the address above

You must not circulate this book in any other form
and you must impose this same condition on any acquirer

Published in the United States of America by Oxford University Press
198 Madison Avenue, New York, NY 10016, United States of America

British Library Cataloguing in Publication Data
Data available

Library of Congress Cataloging in Publication Data
Data available

Extra Series, 114

ISBN 978-0-85-991713-1

Gild of St. Mary, Lichfield.

I. Richard II's Ordinances (A.D. 1387), englisht A.D. 1538.

II. Sir Humfrey Stanley's Ordinances, A.D. 1486.

III. Dean Heywood's Reform of 'Our Lady's Alms-chest,' A.D. 1486.

ORDINANCES OF THE GILD OF ST. MARY, LICHFIELD.[1]

[*Lichfield Gild Register, vellum, leaf* 5, *back.*]
[*Leaves* 1—5 *contain the Latin Charter of Rich. II*, A.D. 1387.]

[A.D. 1538.]

Thys ordinaunce, taken owt of laten in-to englysshe the xiij day of Ianuarye, the xxix yere of o*ur* soue*r*ayne Lord king henry the viij[th], by Rychard Watwode, the*n* being Master of the gild of o*ur* lady and seint Iohn baptist, withe the Consent of m*aste*r Colyns, m[r] Langton, m[r] awsten, m[r] hyll (dyer), m[r] Weston, m[r] orchard, m[r] godfray, m[r] Iordane, m[r] marshall, m[r] stry*n*ge*r*, m[r] byrd, m[r] potte, m[r] bowde, maste*r* bremecham,[2] m[r] hopwoodd, m[r] hyll (m*er*cer), m[r] genyng*es*, m[r] stonyng, m[r] Endesdall, wythe all the other of the xlviij, as here after folowethe, according to the othe whyche we haue taken. /

---

[1] These Ordinances, and those of 1486-7 that follow, have been printed in Harwood's *History of Lichfield*, 1807 ; but as that book is scarce, and probably not in the library of three Members of the Society, Dr. Furnivall took the opportunity of his stay in Lichfield, Aug.—Sept. 1889, to copy the Ordinances from the MS. Gild-Register. Canon Curteis has kindly completed the collation of the 1538 englishing with its Latin, as Dr. F. could not quite finish it.

[2] No doubt he or one of his forefathers came from Bromwicham or Birmingham.

RICHARD II'S GILD-ORDINANCES OF 1387,

ENGLISHT IN 1538.

[*Lichfield Gild Registry, leaf 6.*]

NOBLE kyng Rychard, Second of that name, King of England, in the yere of our Lord M.CCC. lxxxvij, being dysposed and always wyllyng that the honour of godd and the deuocyon of true Chrystyanes shuld encreace and go forward, hathe grauntedd and giuen lycence to Adamare Lychefelde, Thomas Tauerner, Symon Lychefeld, Henry Browne, Robert Tayntrell, Rychard Mortymer, and Davy Brydd, to make a gilde and fraternyte in the towne of Lychefeld, in the honour of godd and the gloryous vyrgin our lady sent Mary, as it appereth more playnly in the seid kinges chartour made for the lycence therof. And so whan the above namedd had opteynedd lycence of the said king, and lycence of the Reuerend fader in god, Lord Rychard, bisshop of Couentre and Lichefeld, the gild began, and was fownded for euer. And they, honorable men, worshypfull men, gentylmen, and many other well disposedd people, began to make them broders and sisters of the said gild; and so thei did choose amonge themself a Master and iiij Wardens for the seyd gild, according to the strength [1] and vertue of the licence of the seid king. And also they made by ther generall consent diuerse

Richard II having, in 1387, licenst 7 citizens to make a Gild of St. Mary in Lichfield, they got the Bp.'s license too, founded the Gild, and elected other Members. Then all chose a Master and 4 Wardens,

[1] Lat. *vim*.

4 Richard II's Gild-Ordinances of 1387; englisht in 1538.

and made their Ordinances:

ordynaunses, whiche be bothe honest and consonaunte to the law, for the establisshment of the seid gild, as it appereth in fourm folowing :

Yearly, on Lady Day,

the Gild shall meet and choose its Master and Wardens.

(1) Fyrst it ys ordenedd that euery yere at the fest of the Conception of our Lady, or within the viij dayes folowing,¹ the broders shall mete, and the master and the wardens² shalbe chosen, so that no man be chosen master or warden ³except he be dwelling within the towne of Lichefeld.³ And if ony man be so chosen master or warden, and they vtterly refuse it, ⁴then lett his name be cancelled and drawen forth of the Regester, and be cownted no more as broder.⁴ And if ony man being master or warden be fownd profytable & fytt for the seid offyce, they may chose him againe whan thei wyll, notwithstanding that thei can not compell him, Except he agreethe to the same election. And the election must be made on thys maner :

Mode of Election:

the old Master names 6 Electors;

they chose 3 others;
[* leaf 6, back]
and these 9, with the 4 Wardens, choose the new Master and Wardens,

by the vote of the majority.

At the day of the election, ⁵whan the master and the wardens and the broders of the seid gild that wylbe at the hall, be gathered together,⁵ The master that was that yere, shall name vj of hys broders of the gild, which shall take to them other iij of ther broders, whom they will, *beside the iiij wardens ; and so thei xiij shal chose one man for master, whom thei think most able and conuenyent, and the iiij wardens, for the prosperous state and conseruation of the seid gild. And for the finall determinacion of the seid election, the gretter part in nomber of the seid xiij shall ratifie and determe the election. Which master and wardens so elect, after that thei haue done ther office by the space

---

¹ uel infra eiusdem festi octabas.
² Custodes.
³⁻³ nisi in dicta uilla Lichefeld connersans pro tempore moram trahat.
⁴⁻⁴ tunc deleatur nomen eius de libro fratrum, & amplius pro fratre minime reputetur.
⁵⁻⁵ Conuenientibus Magistro & custodibus ac fratribus dicte gilde qui interesse uoluerint in loco communi, de die eleccionis premunitis.

of one hoole yere, must make ther accomptes before the broders of the seid gild, of all the commodytes and profyttes to the seid gild belonging for that yere. And if the master or the wardens together, or ony of them by himself, do lend ony mony owt of the comen boxe, Thei shall answer for it at the accomptes, and restore it and repay it to the wardens for the next yere folowing. {Officials render accounts yearly.} {Loans by any singly to be repaid by him.}

(2) Also the ordinaunse is, that the master and wardens¹ shall provyde to make ther accomptes honestly for the yere against the fest of the natiuyte of our lady,¹ or within the viij dayes after the same fest; and euery man entending to be broder shall pay for himself; and then a solempnyte and a fest to be made, in the honour of owr blessed Lady, generally to all broders & sisters of the seid gild, if so be that the master and wardens shall think it so to be most expedyent. {Account-day is Lady-day, when a Feast shall be held.}

(3) Also the ordinaunse is, that all the names of the broders & sisters must be wrytten in a boke made for the same, with ther rewardes and benefytes that thei haue giuen to the seid gild. And whan ony of the broders or sisters dissease,² let the time of hys departing³ be notedd in the same boke, so that ther may be a perpetuall memory of ther departing. {Members' names, gifts, and deaths to be enterd in a Book.}

(4) Also it is ordened that no man shalbe admytt as broder or sister, except it be by the discretion of the master and wardens; nor no man to be admyt, except he be of honest conuersation and good name and fame; and that he giue for the mayntenaunce of the seid gild at his interest or admission,⁴ as he can compownd withe the master and wardens; and then so being admyt, he schall take an othe vpon the evangelist after thys fourm & facion: {Members to be admitted only by the Master and Wardens, who shall fix the admission-fee. All shall take this Oath:}

¹⁻¹ prouideant se ad faciendum liberacionem honorifice de vnica secta erga festum natiuitatis beate marie.
² Lat. ab hac luce migrauerit.
³ obitus.
⁴ ad introitum suum.

6 Richard II's Gild-Ordinances of 1387; englisht in 1538.

[*For the sake of comparison, the earlier text* (A.D. 1387) *is set beside the Hen. VIII. one.*]

[*Oath.* A.D. 1538.]

THE [1]I wilbe faithfull[1] from
OTHE thys time vnto the m*aster*
& broders of the gild of the glorious Virgin Mary of Lichfeld; and I wylbe obedient to them that hereafter shalbe elect to the same, in all thing*es* lefull and honest to be done; [2]and I wyll neue*r* shewe the counsell that the masters or [*leaf*?] wardens shewthe me, for the hurt or damage of ony of them; and if I chaunce to know ony thing which shalbe p*re*iudyciall or hurt[full] to

the seid gild, I will withstond it to the vttermost of my powr.[2] I will obse*r*ue and kepe all ordinaunce*s* that is consonaunte to the law, and made by the m*aster* and wardens for the time being, or here-after to be made, as a brode*r* of the same : so help me godd and the holy evangeliste. /[3]

[*Oath.* A.D. 1387.][4]

I.N. fro þis tyme forwarde, schal be trewe to the Mayste*r* & þe bredren of þ*e* ȝelde of þe gloriouse uirgine marie of lycchefelde : and to hem that schal be in tyme comynge, I schal be obediente i*n* alle leful & honeste þinges to be done. the covnceyl þat the mayste*r* or the wardens schal schewe to me, I schal not telle to no man, in harmyng of hem. ¶ ȝef any þinge truly happon to cum to my knou-lachinge þat schulde turne in-to a notabul hyndringe of þe forsayde ȝelde, or a gret harme, I schal let hyt, or p*ro*cur to be letted, monly[5] aftur my power. ¶ þe ordinaunce acordynge to lawe ordent be þe maystur and þe wardens of the forsayde ȝelde, and to be ordent, as brother of þe same ȝelde I schal kepe truly in myne owne pe*r*son : so helpe me god & the holy gospel !

Adulterers and criminals to be admonisht,

(5) Also the ordinaunce is, that if ony brode*r* of the seid gild b[e][6] co*n*uict of adultery or ony other abhomynable cryme, and so openly diffamed, the m*aster* and wardens shal monysshe h[im] of the same ;

and expeld unless they amend.

and if he wyl not renownse his fawt at the[7] monysshon, but pe*r*seuer and continew in it, Let his nam[e] be cancelled, [8]and that he neuer be admytted afte*r*

[1—1] Ego. N. ab hoc hora inantea, fidelis ero.
[2—2] ad eoru*m* dampnu*m* scienter nemini pandam, Si quid ue*r*o ad meam noticiam deuenire contingat, q*uo*d in notabile detrimentu*m* dicte gilde ue*r*tere posset, seu graue dampnu*m*, impediam uel impedire p*ro*curabo, uirilite*r* iuxta posse. [3] s*an*cta dei eu*an*gelia. [4] Lichfield Gild Register, leaf 15, back.
[5] Lat. *viriliter*.
[6] A strip of the margin is torn off all down the page. [7] MS. the the . .
[8—8] (next page) amplius ad eundem sine noua g*ratia* nullatinus redituris, quia scriptum est : "Deleatur nomen talis malifici," &c.

againe and taken as broder, according to scripture : 'Let the nam[e] of suche an yll lyuer[8] be stryken owt of boke of elect person[es], and not cownted amongest the good men.' And if that ony of the broders or sisters be [1]in ony errour, or ony other detestabl[e] crime,[1] as [2]sone as the master and wardens know it, [2]thei must monysshe the doer charytably, after the sayyng of the gospe[l], "if thy broder do trespas against the, monyssh him that he leve it,"[2] and so forthe. /

<small>Errors to be admonisht charitably.</small>

(6) Also if [3]it chaunce that ony discord or debate be[3] betwyxt any men being broders of the gild, the master and wardens and other of the broders must serche the cawses, [4]and so reforme it, if it can be browght so to passe.[4] Nor one of the broders [5]shall sewe an other broder of the gild,[5] other at the spirituall lawe or temporall, if so be that vnyte and peace may be made betwixt them by the broders of the gild ; nor no man shall seeke or make ony ayde or help of ony stranger against his broder, which is preiudiciall to the gild; for, by that meanes, the gild wyl sone be deprived of the suffrage and profyttes of the same.[6]

<small>All disputes to be settled by the officials.</small>

<small>No outsider to be cald in against a member.</small>

(7) Also it is decreed that all possessyons, goodes, and catell that is giuen to the said gild, to the encrease and sustentacyon of goddes seruyce, [7]shuld be bestowed according to the wyl and mynd of them that giueth it,[7] that thei may be had in perpetuall memorye.

<small>Gifts to be applied as the giver directs.</small>

(8) Also that all men which haue or hold ony tenement of the lettyng of the master and the wardens,

<small>Tenants to honour God first,</small>

[1-1] aliquo errore uel uicio non notorio irretiti.
[2-2] talem delinquentem moneant, iuxta euangelicam ueritatem, Si pecca verit in te frater tuus, &c. a talibus criminibus ut desistant.
[3-3] casualiter exoriri discordiam.
[4-4] si commode fieri poterit, emendetur, inspectis qualitate discordie, & natura. [5-5] fratrem suum suum trahat ad curiam ..
[6] The englisher misunderstood his original: "Nec manutenenciam ab alique domino extraneo aduersus fratrem suum querat, in preiudicium alicuius fratris eiusdem gilde, sub pena priuationis beneficiorum & suffragiorum gilde supradicte."
[7-7] caritatim expendantur uixta uim & effectum uoluntatis donatorum.

fyrst let him pay & do cheef honour to godd̃,[1] and then after to the master and the wardens, according to scripture[2]; "Let thy kyng haue hys seruyce, and thy lord god hys due honour."

and the Gild-Master next.

(9) Also if ony stranger make ony complaynte against a broder of the gild, let then relacyon be made vnto the master and wardens and ther broders; [3]and so when due informacion is had with diligent examinacion, and the truthe knowen, bring the parties together that ther may be made a good end, and discord clene desceedd̃.[3]

Strangers' complaints against Members

to be settled peaceably.

(10) Also it is ordered that if ony broder or sister of the seid gild by misfortune[4] fall to suche pouertie that he hath nothing to help himself, The master and the wardens of the gild must help him[5] as they think best, having respect and consideracion vnto hys old state and cause of hys mysfortune, according to that that godd̃ hath provyded to multyplye the goodes of the seid gild./

Poor Members to be helpt.

(11) Also the ordinaunce is, that no priest shalbe admytt to do seruyce in the seid gild by the desire of ony man, Thowgh the desirer be broder of the seid gild; but that the master and wardens shal admytt the priestes by ther discretion onely; [6]and they shal take as many as shalbe thowght necessary by the most awncyent broders of the gild [6]; and [7]that euery pryest owght to be admytted by the other priestes of the gild; and that thei examyn them surely of ther habylyte so

Priests to be admitted by the

Master and Wardens only,

---

[1] Query, 'do the wonted services due to the chief feudal lord of the land:' Capitali domino seruicia debita & consueta. Canon Curteis thinks the 'scripture' shows that God was meant. [2] iuxta scripturam euangelij.
[3—3] tunc se intromitant diligenter, ut fiat in huiusmodi discordia bonus finis.
[4] per infortunum, absque defectu eiusdem. [5] subueniatur eidem.
[6—6] acceptis sibi tantis quantis sibi uiderint expedire de probabilioribus fratribus.
[7—7] (next page) capellanus qui recipi debeat per alios capellanos eiusdem gilde, de habilitate sua, iusta examinacione probetur antequam admittatur. Ita quod per eorum examinacionem eius habilitas approbetur.

*tha*t thei may be fownd able by ther examynacion⁷; *after examination by the Gild-Priests.*
also that all the priest*es* that be bownd to do ser*u*yce
in the said gild must be honest and of good conue*r*sa-
c*i*on, or ell*es* to haue suffycyent warning, and so de-
pryve the*m* of ther office, and other put in as shalbe
thowght expedyent to the m*as*ter and wardens; and
that the priest*es* of the gild be eue*r*y day in the churche *The Gild-Priests to help the Parish Priests in divine service.*
of o*ur* lady at the divyne se*r*uys, that by ther helpe the
p*ar*yssh pryest*es* may ¹the better do dyvyne se*r*uys to
the hono*ur* of god.¹

(12) Also it is decreedd that one of the priest*es* of *One priest to be Clerk of the Gild,*
the gild shalbe made by the m*as*ter and wardens Clerk
of the gild, ²to wryte and note² all p*r*ofyttes and rentes *and keep its accounts,*
belonging to the seid gild, and also expens*es* and
charg*es*. And the same priest so elect shal shew to the
m*as*ter and wardens how long *he will continew in the [* leaf 8]
seid office; and hys felows shalbe ³at hys assigning³ in
doing ther dutie or office in the Churche. In conside*r*-
ac*i*on wherof the m*as*ter and wardens shall giue him by *for 6s. 8d. a year.*
the yere ⁴for his paines taking,⁴ vj s viij d ./

(13) Also it is ordeined that all the priest*es* of the *All Gild-Priests to be at Our Lady's Mass in the Church in the Market-place.*
seid gild shalbe att o*ur* lady masse, and at antem ⁵that
is called Salue,⁵ in the Chapell of o*ur* lady standing in
the markett place of Lich*f*eld, except they be lett by a
reasonable cause; ⁶and that eue*r*y of them shal depose
for an other, conce*r*ning honest conue*r*sat*i*on and gr*au*yte
of mane*r*s./

(14) Also the ordinaunce is, that all the pryest*es* *All Gild-Priests to sleep in*
of the seid gild be down-lyyng and vprysing in ther
Chambers⁶ apoynted to them by the m*as*ter and his

¹⁻¹ gloriosius ad laudem dei possint p*er*fice*r*e.   ²⁻² et scribat.
³⁻³ ad ejus innitac*i*onem.   ⁴⁻⁴ iuxta eius me*r*itum.
⁵⁻⁵ que dicitur Salue regina.
⁶⁻⁶ This clause belongs, in the Latin, to the subsequent ordinance, and runs thus: Item c*um* solitarius ceciderit, no*n* habeat sublevante*m*; et ut quilibet eor*um* sit alteri*us* testis idoneus super conue*r*sacione honesta mor*um*que gr*au*itate, ordinatum est q*uod* om*n*es capellani .. sint iacentes et leuantes in cameris iuxta capellam.

broders, that be buyldec beside the chapeH of our lady
in Lich*feld* within a ce*r*taine hows, calledd ' the pries*tes*
hall,' a-pointed for them.[1] [2]And that they bord together,[2] except a reasonable cause or bodely infirmyte
which ther felows knowth, do let them; and if ony of
the seid pryes*tes* do withdraw him-self from his company, [3]or make mery with ony other ma*n*[3] within the
Cyte of Lich*feld* for the space of iij or iiij or v daies
or an hoole weeke, he shall pay the cos*tes* of his
comens neuertheles./

<small>the Priests' Hall, and board together.</small>

<small>If any doesn't,</small>

<small>he shall still pay his share.</small>

(15) Also it is ordeined that the Clark for the time
being in the said chapeH having the office of a decane,
by the voluntary rewar*des* and goodnes of the towne-
dwellers and brod*ers* & sis*ters* of the sayd gild, [4]shall
be eue*ry* day[4] at our lady masse and antem that we call
"Salue," Except he be let w*ith* a reasonable cause.

<small>The Clerk and Deacon of the Chapel</small>

<small>shall attend daily Mass.</small>

(16) Also whan Phylyp Stretehay,[5] m*aster* of the
gild, and Roger Ridware, Thomas Wysse, Rychard
Chamber and Rychard Cowpe*r*, wardens of the same
gild, with consent of the other broders, did admytt
Will*iam* Wylnehale, priest, to be one of the pres*tes* of
the gild as to a pe*r*petuyte, as it apperethe in his
wryting made therof, and sealed with the Comen seale,
for the whych admyssyon the seid Wyllyam was bownd
by the seid m*aster* and wardens to wryte and cast ther
accomp*tes* yerely, wha*n* the wardens for the time being
shuld com*m*and him, [6]and to wryte ther names pa*r*-
ticulerly that do take the accomp*tes*, and to make the
wardens pa*r*fyt in such thing*es* as belongeth to the
seyd gild./[6]

<small>Wm. Wylnehale has been appointed permanent keeper of the Gild's accounts.</small>

[1] See p. 14, no. 13, below.
[2]–[2] et in quadam aula .. su*m*ptib*us* com*m*unib*us* simul comedant et co*n*-
uesca*n*t.
[3]–[3] vel eciam conuiuare c*um* aliquo alio.
[4]–[4] assiduus sit.
[5] Philippus de Strethay.
[6]–[6] et no*m*ina huiusmodi libr*a*cione*m* recipientium p*a*rticulari*ter* conscri-
bendi, dic*t*isqu*e* Custodibus qu*a*ndo requisitus fue*r*it intimandi.

Lichfield Gild Register, leaf 8, back.

SIR HUMFREY STANLEY'S ORDINANCES FOR THE GILD.

A.D. 1486-7.

In the fest of sent mychell tharcangell, The yere of owre soueraine Lord, King Henry the vij[th], the second, By the hyghe consideraci*on* of the right worshipfull Syr Humfrey Stanley, knight, the m*aster* of the gild, and the worshipfull his brothers, in eschewing of grett inco*n*venyence and malyce, haue ordened and constitute vpon certaine articles for the worship of the Citie, vnite, pease, and welfare of the Cominalte./

(1.) *Unity to be kept among the* 48 *Members.*

Fyrst, it is ordened that the m*as*ter of the gild, w*ith* the xlviij, shal stedfastly abyde together in one as in all, as they and eche of the*m* p*er*sonally made there othe solemply apon a boke in p*er*forming the same, and to se good rule be kept, and pease to be had, for the worship of the seid cyte, & welfare of the comminalte.

(2.) *Disputes to be settled by the Master and Brothers.* *Disobedients to be expeld.*

Also it is ordened that if ony vnkindely, or ony caus vnkindely to be giuen in deling amongest the seid xlviij, that then the knowlege therof cu*m* to the m*as*ter, he and his brothers here the mat*er* and cawses betwixt them; and the p*ar*ties to abyde the rule, arbiterment and award of the seid m*as*ter and his brothers. And the seid p*ar*ties so moved wyl not abide the ordina*u*nce of the seid m*as*ter and his brothers, they to be kept owt of the worshipfull elecc*io*n and fraternyte of the seid Cyte, and neu*er* to cu*m* amongest them to noo Councell, but be discharged as a ma*n* forsworne openly and audyently vpon a boke./

(3.) *Fine for not attending Meetings. Expulsion after three defaults.*

Also it is ordened that as ofte as the m*a*ster of the gild, his brothern and the xlviij, haue mate*r* of co*m*municac*i*on, and assigned to mete at the haℓℓ of o*u*r lady, or at any other place, the day and how*r* prefixed; and vpon the same, the xlviij so warned, if ony of them wi*th*draw themself, and wyl not cu*m* at the instaunce of the seid m*a*ster and brother*n* (wi*th*owt caus resonable) shal pay and giue iiij d to be put iu-to the boxe tyl the accomp*tes*, and then it to be devyded after the discret*i*on of the m*a*ster of the gild and the xlviij. And if the seid p*er*son or p*er*sons wyl absent them-self from the seid m*a*ster and his brother*n* an-other time, after resonable warn-yng [leaf 9] shal pay ij pownd of wax; and as ofte as ony of th*em* so fawteth after iij times monysshed, to be discharged and put owt, after the forme a-fore rehersedd./

(4.) 24*d*. *Fine for bloodshed in Frays. Surety for keeping the Peace.*

Also it is ordenedd, that as ofte as ony frayes be made, and blood-shed vpon the same, both p*a*rties so disposed, The C*o*nstables to take the*m* to ward to the gayle haℓℓ, and ther to find sufficient suerte for the peace, and vp*o*n ther good abering, or they dep*a*rt, for ony fauo*u*r or love of kynseme*n* or frend*es*. And the p*a*rties to pay for the seid fraye and bloodshed, to the Come*n* box*e* .xx d., and to the Constable iiij d, as oft as ony such frays be made, what p*er*son or p*er*sons so-eue*r* thei be, the p*re*sentment by the xij me*n*, and the furrers[1] of the court, vnto my lord reservedd notwithstondinge./

(5.) 16*d*. *Fine for less Frays, with Surety for Peace thereafter.*

Also it is ordened that, as often as ony frays or stryes[2] be made, or drawing vnlawfuℓℓ wepons in malyce, in sturring *and* fering the people, The Constables to take the*m* to ward, and ther to find suffi-cient surete according a-fore rehersed, and to pay for the fray xij d to the boxe, and to the Constable iiij d, The p*re*sentment to my Lord reservedd./

[1] '*Fourreur*, a Forager,' or '*Fourier:* n. An Harbinger.'—1611. Cotgr.; or '*Furer*. An officer whose duty it was to burn false measures.'—Dean Milles' MS. in Halliwell's Gloss.

[2] ? for stryfes.

(6.) *Night-walkers and Rioters to be arrested, admonisht, expeld, or put in Prison.*

Also it is ordened that, if ther be ony misruled and ill-disposed person or persons within the Citie, that suspeciously walketh by night, owt of due time, keping alehowses in ryott and mysdoing in trobeling ther neyghbours, The Constables to take them to ward, vntyll the master of the gild and his brothers take them owt, and so monysshe them to leve suche rule and mysgyding, or elles to voyd the Citie, or elles to be taken to pryson.

(7.) *Harlots to be set on the Cuckstool, and expeld the City.*

Also it is ordened, if ther be ony misruled woman of hyr body, that is called a comen synner with euery person that wil dispose himself to medle with such,—whereby may grow, & doth growe, in diuerse parties, greate mischef, as well by [leaf 9, back] murder[1] of men, as to the greate displeasure of god, and greate ieopardy of euerlasting paine,—Such openly knowen (the ponisshment of the Church reserved), that they, the Constables, to take them and sett them vpon the Cookstole, ther openly schamed, and to voide the towne, vpon paine of prysonment./

(8.) *Scolds to be warnd; and on their 3rd default, set on the Cuckstool.*

Also it is ordened that, if ther be ony woman that is a comen scold, that by her euyl tong and sclaunder may grow myschef and troble amongest neighbours, The Constable shal cum to that person or persons, charging them, in the name of the master of the gild and hys brothern, to leve ther malice & euyll tonges; ij times so monisshed; and if she wil not be ruled, she to be had to the cookestole, ther to be knowen in the example of other /

(9.) *Disputes between Members' servants to be settled by the Master, &c.*

Also it is ordenedd that, if it happen, and as ofte as it happeneth, ony vnkindnes or frayes made betwene ony seruaunte or seruauntes of the xlviij, the mater & cawses shalbe reserued to the master of the gild and his brothern: the masters of the parties notwithstanding to be ruledd by the seid master and his brothern./

[*Three more Articles follow, in a rather later* 16*th-cent. hand, and different ink.*]

[1] MS. by murder.

14 *Gild-Ordinances added to Sir Humfrey Stanley's, ab. 1500.*

(10.) *Gild tenants to pay rent duly. No tenant-at-will to underlet.*

Also it is ordenyd that euery tenand that holdythe any landis or tenymentis of the Gild, to paye ther Rentis at ther acustumyd days, or within one monythe then nexte foloyng; and that no tenaind at wyll shall make a tenand.

(11.) *Masters to keep the Ordinances, or be fined.*

Item, it ys a-greyde by Richarde Wetwode, then beyng Master of our ladys gylde, with the consent of all the hall, that the seyd Master and his successouris, and the xlviij, shall well and trully ffolowe and kepe all & singullare ordinancis conteynyde in thys Regester; and for euery defalt, to paye ther mercyment.

(12.) *All Deeds to be registerd in English.*

Item, it ys a-Greyde that all Indenturis of our ladys landys shalbe sene, & the same to be regesterd in Englishe.

[*leaf* 10: in the same or a contemporary hand.]

Item, the Taske of Lichfelde ys ... ... xij li vj s viij d

(13.) *The Priests'-Hall Statutes to be in English.*

Item, it ys a-Greyde that the Statutis be-longyng to the prestis hall[1] shalbe draue owt in-to Englyshe, and to be delyuerde to the Comenaris ther.

(14.) *Date for St. Michael's Churchwardens' Accounts.*

Item, it ys a-Greyde that the churche-wardens of Seint Michaellis shall make ther accompt the sondaye next aftyr the fest of the purificacion of our blessed lady[2] nex[t] aftyr theye be owt of ther offecis, vppon payn of forfettyng xx s. to be payd to the Reparacion of the same churche.

(15.) *Date for Stowe Churchwardens' Accounts.*

Item, that the Churche-wardens of Stowe,[3] shall make ther a-compt the secunde sondaye next folloyng the seyd fest of purificacion next aftyre the[y] be owt of offecis, vppon lyke payne.

(16.) *Date for St. Mary's Churchwardens' Accounts.*

Item, the churche-wardens of our ladys, that they shall make ther a-compt the thryde sondaye next aftyr the seyde fest of purificacion next aftyr they be owt of offece, vppon lyke payne.

[1] See p. 10, art. 14, above.   [2] Feb. 2.   [3] A parish close to and N.E. of Lichfield.

(17.) *Gild-Masters to wear Scarlet Gowns when warnd so to do.*

Item, it ys a-Greyde that the Master of the Gilde, and all other that haue byn Masteris of the same Gilde, shall were ther skarlett Gownys the days next folloyng' that they haue monyshion by the bell-man ouer Evyn, vppon payn of euery offender for euery defalt ... ... xij d̃ to be payd to the comyn box of the hall. _{pri[n]cipel Festis}

And yff the Master of the Gilde for that tyme beyng' Gyff them not warnynge accordyng' as ys a-boue seyd, that then the seyd Master shall forfet to the seyd boxe, for euery defalt ... ... ij s

[*leaf 10, back, in another hand.*]

A.D. 1538.

EXPULSION FROM THE GILD, OF WILLIAM STONDE-NOGHT, FOR REFUSING TO SERVE AS MASTER.

For so Muche as it ys enactyde of olde tyme, as playnly doythe apere [by] the ordinances Establyshyde by the graunt of the Nobyll kyng' Richarde, the secunde of that name, that euery yere, at the Fest of the Concepcion of our blessyd lady / or within viiij dayes then nexte Followyng', the Masteris and bretherne shall mett in the Comyn hall / and ther a Newe Master and wardens shalbe chosyn / and yff any Man be so Chosyn Master or warden / and that he or they vttyrly refuse it / then hys Name to be cansellyde, and drawne Forthe of the Register, and to be acomptyde No more as a brother / accordyng' to whiche ordinance, the Master and bretherne in the Fest of the seyde concepcion of our lady in the xxx^{ti} yere of the Reyng' of our suffaryng lorde kyng henry the viijth, to thentent that a Newe Master to be made, accordyng' to ther olde Custum / dyde assembyll ther selfis in the seyde place / and all thyngis requisyde to that eleccion obseruyde, dyde Elect, nominate and chuse Wyllyam̃ Stondenoght, a brother of the seyde Gilde, to be Master of the same / whiche William so electe, namyde & chossyn, hath Contemptuusly and vtterly refusyde the same / Contrary to the ordinance afforeseyde / and hys othe here-to-fore in that behahalf' made / ther-fore the olde Master for that tyme beyng', with the consent of all his seyde Bretheris, the xv[th] daye of December' then) nexte ensuyng' the seyde Fest [leaf 11] of Concepcion) the yere a-boue wryttyn), accordyngly to ther seyde statutis, dyde Cansell and drawe Forthe owt of the Regester' Booke, and by the3 presentis do Cansell and drawe Forthe the Name of the seyde William, and neuer here-aftyr to be reputyde and takyn) for a brother of the seyde Gilde, Ne to enjoye any pryvy-lege, emolumentis or profettis, apertenyng' or in any wyse belongyng to the same.

[? In another 16th-century hand.]

A.D. 1539.

FOR THE A-COMPT OF THE MASTER OF THE GILDE.

Memorandum, that hit ys a-Greyde by the Master of the Gildes[1] and his bretherne, that the seyde Master & his iiij wardens, and ther Successouris, Shall make ther a-Compte vppon) Mydlent Sondaye next aftyr that they shalbe owte of ther offecis, vppon) payn) of for-fetyng' xl s, the whiche xl s to be levyde, xiij s iiij d of the seyde Master, and xxvj s viij d of the seyde iiij warde[ns], that ys to wyt, euery one of the seyde wardens, vj s viij d; and the seyde forfet to be a-pleyde to the commyn) Taxe of Gilde hall. anno Rengni Regis henrici octaui xxx°. (22 April 1538 to 21 April 1539.)

[leaf 12, back, in another hand, of Philip and Mary's reign.]

LEVY OF A FIFTEENTH FROM LICHFIELD.

(A.D. 1558) The taske[2] of the Citie of Lichfeld is xij li.

In primis, Bore Strete[3]	xx s ij d
Item, Sadlers Strete[4]	xlix s

[1] ? MS. Gilded.
[2] Tax.
[3] parallel with Market St. The post-office and police-court are in it.
[4] now Market Street, at right angles to Bird Street.

1558. *Levy of a Fifteenth from Lichfield.*

Item, Birde Strete¹ and Sandforde Strete	... ...	xxxix s
Item, Bekon Strete²	...	xxviij s
Item, Tamworth Strete³	...	xx s
Item, grene hill⁴	...	xv s
Item, Stowe Strete⁵		xxijs iiij d
Item, Cundith Strete⁶		xxxiij s vj d
Item, Wade Strete⁷	...	ix s
Item, saint Johns Strete⁸		xviij s vj d

12 ti 15 s' 6 d   The tenor of the billettes Directed to the Dus-
12 ti 15 s' 6 d   siners⁹ in euery seuerall warde for the colleccion
               off the sommes abouc written //

To the Dussiners of Sadlers strete.¹⁰

We will and commande you, in the King and Quenes magesties names, for to levy and Gather in your ward, the xvth graunted to their gracis Vse, with all spede.

              Edmunde Bardell ⎫
              John Dyott   ⎬ Bayliffes

[These men are enterd as Bailiffs in 1558, in a later leaf of the MS, in the George Bagshawes' 'Catalogue of all the Baylyffes and Sheriffes that haue bene in ye cytty of Lichfeld sythynce the Incorporation therof.' Harwood, in his *History of Lichfield*, 1807, p. 220, in his print of this Catalog, claims this John Dyott, or his namesake, nephew of Sir —— Dyott, as Shallow's 'little John Doit of Staffordshire,' in 2 *Henry IV*, III. iii.—F.]

   ¹ leading to Stafford. Sandford St. runs out of it on the West.
   ² Beacon St. continues Bird St., runs up Beacon Hill, and is part of the Stafford Road.
   ³ runs from Bore St. to Green Hill.
   ⁴ A street leading up to St. Michael's Church (on the hill), and down to the Trent Valley station.
   ⁵ runs N.E. out of Tamworth St. to Stowe.
   ⁶ runs from Bore St. to the east end of the Cathedral.
   ⁷ runs out of St. John's St. parallel to Market St. and Bore St. farther south.
   ⁸ Continues Bird St., and runs into the Tamworth and London Road.
   ⁹ the 12 Reserve-constables.
   ¹⁰ now Market Street.

[*No break in the MS.*]

(*The last document in the Lichfield Gild Registry: leaves not numberd.*)

A.D. 1486. Dean Heywood's Reform of the administration of "Our Lady's Alms-Chest," or "Herwood's & Radclyf's Coffers": £40 for Loans to the Poor of Lichfield (£7 now given by Dean Heywood).

Ihesus.

I, Dean Heywood,

To all cristen people that this present writing shall se or here, Thomas Heywood, bachiler of both lawes:[1] Dean of the cathedral churche off Lich*feld*, sendeth helth in our lord euerlasting!

In my Visitation on Nov. 22, 1485,

Be it knowen vnto yowe, that we, in owr ordinary visitac*io*n had and exercysed in the chapell of owr lady beside the market place of Lichfeld, the xxij day of nouember, the yere of owr lord M CCCC lxxxv, among other crymes and defaw*tes* then shewed and detected to

found

vs, We fownd that, wher the worshipfull men, m*aster* Ioan Herwood and m*aster* George Radclyf, somtime chanons residencyeres in the seid cath*edral* church of Lich*feld*, ordeyned too chestes in the forseyd chapell of

that £20 was given by Jn. Herwood

owr lady, in one of the which chestes the seyd m*aster* Joan Herwood put xx li, and in the other chest the

and also £20 by George Radclyf, (each in a chest,) to help the poor of Lichfield.

seid m*aster* George Radclyf put other xx li of lawfull money of England, to be conue*r*ted to the behofe, profytte, and releving of poore people of the seid citie

[1] Canon and civil.

1486. Dean Heywood's Reform of 'Our Lady's Alms-Chest.'

of lich*feld*, and thervpon disposed and ordeyned in ther last willes vnder certaine mane*rs*, fourmes, and condicions, as in ther writing*es* thervpon made, more plainly apperyth, the teno*ur* wherof folowethe in these wordes:

[*Canon Radclyf's Regulations for administering his Gift of* £20 *to* "*Our Lady's Alms-Chest,*" *or* "*Herwood's Coffer.*" Febr. 1457.]

In the name of god, amen! For as moch as Ioan Herwood, late chanon of the cathedrall church of lich*feld*, haue fownded a certaine almes chest in owre lady chapell, called the chapell church, beside the market place of the citie of lich*feld*, vnto the releef of pooremen in the seid citie, and in V. prebendes of the same, which chest is called "owr ladies almes chest," or otherwise " Herwodes cofre," In the which he put xx ƚi of lawfull money of englond, and set forth and ordeyned diue*rs* ordinaunces[1] for the conse*r*uacion, as well of the money as of the cawcyons and pledg*es* leyd in the seyd chest, I, George Radclyf, chanon of the cathedrall church aforeseyd, and late archedecane of Chestre, haue ordeyned an other cofre, and haue put in hyt xx ƚi sterling, for thentent that poore men dwelling wit*h*in the citie aboueseid, and the subarbes of the same, (and not wit*h*owt the citie or subarbes,) may be releeved by a sufficient gage or pledge leyd in-to the seyd cofre for borowing mony of the same; which cofre shalbe calledde " Radclyffes cofre," by this p*r*ovision :

(1) That the master of the gilde in the citie aboveseid, the Sacristan of the mynester, the warden of the chapell church, and our priest which the master of the gild and his bretherne do trust most sure, may be kepers of the kayes of the seid cofre, for the conse*r*uacion, as well of the money, as of the gag*es* or pledg*es* to be leid in the same. And that euery of them haue a kaye by themself, that the money and pledg*es* of the seyd cofre may be well kept, oneles that ony hurt or hinderaunce maye chaunce to the cofre for defawt of safe custody.

(2) Farthermore I haue ordeyned and apoynted that no man shall borowe aboue xx s at one time, and

Canon Radclyf's Will or Deed recites Canon Herwood's gift,

£20 in "Our Lady's Alms-Chest or Herwood's Coffer,"

and says that he, Canon Radclyf, has put another £20 in another chest, "Radclyf's Coffer,"

to be lent to poor men of Lichfield.

the kepers of the kayes are the Gild-Master and 3 other men, to keep the money and the securities for loans.

what ye may borow at ones.

---
[1] Not now known to be.

what pledge.	that but for one half yere; and that he lay in a gage or pledge better then the money so borowed by iij s iiij d./ And that the gage or pledge must be gold, syluer, tyn, brasse, [*new leaf*] lead, pewter or yron, and that it be taken by wayght, in no wyse regarding the fourme or facion of the gage or pledge.
how to order the pledge forfeted.	(3) Also if the gage or pledge so leyd in the seyd cofre be not redemed at the half yeres end, and the hoole som of the money borowed owt of the cofre be not repayed, then the gage or pledge must be sold; and the one half off the mony passing the valour of the gage, must be delyuered to the owner, the other half to be put to the augmentacion of the sayd cofre; So that in no wyse the seyd cofre, with money aforseid, can cum to decaye or hinderaunce.
a man can borow but ones in the yere	(4) And if ony man borow money vpon a gage or pledg for one half yere, he shall borow no more vnto that seid yere be fully ended and past, oneles that an other man having as moch nede as he, can not be eased and helped with so moch mony vpon a gage as the other had before.
The office of the kepers	(5) And that the seid master of the gild, and his successors being masters of the gild, and the warden of the chapell church, being too kepers of the cofre, shall delyuer the other too kepers (being present) at the end of ther accomptes, the kayes of the cofre, and goodes being in the same, with the money, the gages and pledges, and the names of them that hath borowed, and the day of rescyving the money by Indentures made to the master of the gild and the warden of the church for the time being, the other too kepers also being present. And that the gages or pledges so delyueredd to the kepers of the kayes may be alwayes kept within the foreseid cofre.
Too of the kepers be chosen euery yere.	(6) And so euery master of the gild, and the warden of the chapell church for the time being, shall alwayes reseyve of ther precessors the kayes, with the Indentures, of the seid cofre, and syxe honest, discrete, and most sufficient burgeces, bretherne of the gild, be present at the sight of the seid cofre, and delyueraunce of the seyd kayes, oneles that by covyne or euyll dispocicion (which god forbeed!) the cofre, with money and gages or pledges in the same, be conveyed away or dispoyled by ony other meanes; but that the seyd cofre with money may be ordered and disposed vnto the releef and ayde of poore folkes, according to the ordinaunce above specyfied.

(7) Provided alway that the Sacristen of the mynster for the time being may kepe alway one kaye of the cofre, and all other ordinaunces that the seyd master Ioan Herwood haue made discretely and wysely at the day of the ordinaunce of the seid cofre, which do not repunge to this ordinaunce. I wille that my ordinaunces be referred to those, except the provysions and ordinaunces aboveseid. Dated and delyuered by my executours, at the gild hall, the saturday next after the purificacyoue of our lady, the xxxv yere of the reigne of king Henry the syxte after the conquest. *The Minster Sacristan may keep one key of the Coffer.*

Febr. 1457.

But for as moche as we haue lerned and fownd, not onely of faythfull relacion, but also by the openes off the dede, that the seid summe of xl li put in the seid chestes as ys aforeseid, by vnhedynes, blame, and neglygens of kepers of the kayes of the seid chestes before times passed, ys now diminysshed and wel nygh wasted and peyred, So that at the time of owr seid visitacion ther was no money found in the seyd chestes, nor Iuelles or weddes ouer the summe of xiij li, vnto great hinderaunce, hurt, and preiudyce of the poore people of the seid citie, sclaunder and peryll of the sowles of the seid kepers of the kayes, breking the ordinaunces and last willes of the seid worshipfull men, master Ioan and master George, and also shrewd example to all other Christen people, *Now I found that, by the negligens of kepers the £40 had come down to only £13, in money and securities.*

Wherupon, we, considering that[1] apperteyneth to owr ordinary cure, to fauour and norysshe the thinges that be rightfull,—and the thinges that letten the profyt of vertues, to correct and amend,—as moche as in vs ys; We therfore, couetinge due reformacion to owr powr to be had in the premisses, by lawfull processe and by laborous and diligent inquisicion and examinacion, haue found and geten xx li, being in diuers mennes handes, not lykely to haue ben recouered; the which summe of xx li, with the forseid summe of xilj li, making the summe of xxxiij li, We, be owr *Inquisition of the Deane.*

But I have routed out £20 more in divers men's hands,

making a total of £33,

---

[1] That it.

ordinary power and auctoryte, and also by the will, consent and assent of William Rokeley, now being master of owr Lady of Lichefeld, and of other worthy, good and honest men, accustomed to haue rule of the seid gild, haue made and ordeyned to be put and keped from hensforth, in one chest, vnder the maner and fourme in the ordinaunce of the seid master George above expressed.

<small>and I have orderd this to be kept in one chest.</small>

But for as moch as, of the seid summe of xl li giuen and graunted by the seid master Ioan and master George (as it is before rehersed), the summe of vij li ys vtterly wasted and loste by the negligence of kepers of the kayes beforetime, So that now it can not be knowen nor fownd in ony wyse in whose handes yt restythe, We therfore, the Deane of the seyd cathedrall churche, —for the helth of owr soule, and for the wele and profit of the pore people of Lichfeld aforeseid, and also that the last willes and ordinaunces of the forseid master Ioan and George hereafter may be duly obserued and kept, coueting and willing to fulfill, renew, and make hoole the seid summe off xl li,—We haue yeuen, graunted and delyuered the summe of vij li of lawfull money of Englond, of owr owne proper goodes, to be disposed in all maner wise after the fourme, strength and effecte of the ordinaunces of the seyd master George; and haue made and ordeyned the seid vij li to be put and kept in the seid chest with the seid summe of xxxiij li, for the which thing the master, the wardens, and the most worthy and worshipfull brether of the seyd gild, in ther name, and of other ther bretherne of the same,—moved of veray charite, and coueting spirituall giftes to be yelded for the seid temporall goodes yeuen and graunted by the seid master Ioan and master George, and also by vs, as ys before rehersed,— wyll, ordeyn and graunt that, as oftimes as the foure kayberers or ther deputies, and the seid borowers and

<small>And as £7 of the money is clean gone,</small>

<small>I've made it good</small>

<small>the hole summe of xl li repared.</small>

<small>And I've orderd this £7 to be put with the £33 in the said one chest,</small>

<small>and that its 4 Key-bearers</small>

refoorers, and eueryche of them, shall deuoutly say before the highe auter, or som other auter next to the seid chest, a pater noster and aue maria [*next leaf*] For the helthe of the soules of the seid master Ioan and master George, and of oure soule, the Deane aforeseid, and that all the ordinaunces, willes and grauntes of the seid master Ioan and master George, owres, and other as above, ben had and made hereafter, more straitly, more diligently and effectually be obserued and kepte, We,—bi oure ordinary powre and auctoryte, and with and of the will, consent and assent of the most worthy, worshipfull and honest men of the seid Citie, brethern of the seid gild,—make and ordeyne, that from hensforth euery keper of the kayes of the seid chest, in the beginning of his office shal swere vpon a boke,—before the Deane of the seid cathedrall churche for the time being (or suche as shalbe in his steade), and also before the wardens and other vj worshipfull and honest men, brether of the seide gild,—that he shall truely obserue and kepe, for his time, all and singuler ordinaunces, willes and grauntes aboueseid, in all maner of thinges after his powre; as in lykewise William Rokeley, now being master of the seide Gilde, Syr Ioan Paxon, Sacristen of the seid cathedrall church, Syr Nycolas Appulton, pryst of the seid gild, and Robert worth,[1] otherwise called Buggyn, warden of the seyd chapell, now kepers of the seyd kayes, haue sworne, and euery of them haue sworne, vpon a boke before vs, Deane aforeseid, and a great multitude of people being present in the seid chapell, and haue taken vpon them wilfully the charge of such maner keping.

Moreouer we will and ordeyne that in euery visitacion to be had and exercysed herafter in the seid chapell of our ladye, in oure time, or in time of Deanes

shall more strictly keep the Regulations of Canons Herwood and Radclyf.

And that every Key-keeper shall swear to keep the said Regulations truly.

The 4 Key-keepers are Gild-master Rokeley, Sacristan Paxon, Gild-priest Appleton, and Chapel-Warden Worth (or Buggyn).

And I order that at every Visitation,

---

[1] The scribe first wrote "wortherwise," and then "worth" over the line.

special enquiry shall be made into the keeping of these Regulations,

oure successors for time being, amonge other, speciall and diligent inquisicio*n* to be made of obse*r*uing and keping of all the forseid statu*tes*, willes and ordinaunc*es*. And yf ther be ony thing therof omytted or lost, or not performed or fulfilled, then we will and ordeyne

and all abuses reformd.

that due reformac*i*on be made in that behalf, by the deane of the seid cathedrall churcĥ for the time being, to the pleasure of almyghtie god, and to the behofe and p*r*ofyt of the pore people dwelling in Lichfeld aforeseid.

Also, that one copy of the Trust-Deed be kept in the Alms-Chest, and one in the Cathedral Treasury.

Furthermore we will and ordeyne that the one parte of the Indentures hereoff made, remayne in the forseid chest, and the other parte remayne in the treasure-house of the seid cathedrall church, for the more suretie, that in case doutfull or opinab'e [? questiones aryse], (which, god forbede!) recourse may be had thither for a certaynte to be had in the same. In faith and witnes of the which all singuler forseid thing*es*, at the request and instance of the master and wardens of the seid gild, and of many other moste worthy and worshipfull of comynalte of the seid cite, as well the seale of the office of owr Deanry which we vse in this behalf, as the come*n* seale of the seid gild, ben put to the seid

Seald, 1 June, 1486.

indentures. Youen, as to sealing of the same, the first day of the moneth of Iune, the yere of oure lord .M.CCCC. lxxxvj./

FIRST EXTANT CHARTER OF THE LICHFIELD TAILORS.

6 April. 18 Elizabeth. A.D. 1576.

To all Chrystian people to whome this present wrytinge shall come, gretyng in our lord god everlastinge! Knowe ye, that whereas in the Parlyament holden at Westmynster the xxvth day of Ianuarie in the nynetenthe yere of the Reingne of our late soveraigne lorde of famous memorye, Kynge Henry the seventhe[1] [A.D. 1504], it was inacted, ordeyned, and establisshed by our saide soveraigne lorde, by the advise and consent of the lordes Spyrytuall and Temporall, and the Commons of the saide Parlyament assembled, and by the aucthoritee of the same, that no masters, wardens and Felowshippes, craftes or mysteries, or any of them, nor any[2] Rulers of Guyldes or Fraternyties, should from thereforthe take vppon them to make any actes or ordynaunces, nor to execute any actes or ordynaunces by them afore that tyme made, or att any tyme then to come to be made, in disherytaunce or dymynucion of the kinge his prerogatyve, or of any other, nor against the common proffyte of the people, but if the same actes or ordynaunces were examyned or approved by the Chaunceller Tresorer of England, or Cheeffe Justices of either Benche, or three of them, of beffore bothe the Justices of Assise in theyr circuyte and progresse in

In 1504, Parliament

enacted (by 19 Hen. VII, c. 7)

that no Crafts should thenceforth make any Ordinances

except with the approval of (among others) Two Judges of Assise.

[1] The Act 'against making private and unlawful Statutes by Corporations' recites as its cause the expired Statute, 15 Hen. VI, c. 6, against Gilds &c. making 'many and unreasonable Ordinances, as well in Prices of Wares as other Things, for their own singular Profit, and to the common Hurt and Damage of the People.'   [2] ? nor any.

the Shere where suche actes & ordynaunces be made, vppon payne of forfeyture of Fortie pounde for every tyme that they doe the Contrarye, as in the saide acte more playnely dothe and may appeare, Nowe the Baylieffes and Cytezens, and the Master, Wardens and Combretheren of the mystery, crafte, and Scyence of the Taylers of the Citie of Lichffelde, willyng and desyringe the saide acte in euerye behalfe to be observed and kept, and the auncyent and lawdable customes vsed in the foresaide Cittie, tyme out of mynde, to be revyved, exercysed and put in vse, the sixthe day of Apryll, in the eigtenthe yere of the Raigne of oure Soveraigne Ladie Elizabethe, by the grace of god, of England, Fraunce and Irelande, quene, defender of the Faithe, &c., haue exhybyted and presented there humble petycion and request vnto vs, Edwarde Saunders Knyght, Lorde Cheefe Baron, and William Lovelace, Sericante att Lawe, Justices of Assize, within the country of Stafforde, with a booke conteynynge dyverse statutes, actes, and Ordynaunces devysed, ordeyned and made for the felowshippe of Taylers and there successors in the said Cittie, and for the common wealthe and conservacion (?) of the good and prosperous estate of the same misterye, and for the Better Rules, constytucions and ordynaunces of the same Felowshippe establysshed, ordeyned and vsed for the foresaide felowshippe of Taylors within the said Cittie of lichfelde, the libertyes, subburbes, and precynte of the same; And therevppon, hime instant, he desyred vs that we, all and euery the saide statutes, ordynaunces and Rules by the foresaid Bayliffes, Cytezens, Masters, Wardens, Combretheren and Felowshippe aforesaide and there predecessors, to the foresaide intent made, ordeyned and establyssed, would oversee, examyne, correcte and amend after suche manner' and forme as the saide acte of Parlyamente rehersethe,

The Citizens

and Tailors of Lichfield

have now petitiond us, the Lord Chief Baron and Justice Lovelace (2 Judges of Assise), and shown us a new Book of Ordinances for the Lichfield Tailors,

and kave askt us

to examine it.

Lichfield Tailors. First Ordinances, 1576.

We, well prooeyvinge the saide supplycacion, and wayinge the petycion and desyeres in the same to vs given by the saide acte of Parlyament, Doe approve, ratifie, and allow all and singuler the actes, ordynaunces, statutes and Rules by the foresaide Baylieffes, Citezens, Master, Wardens, Combretheren and Felowshippe of the Taylers made, ordeyned and appoynted, the Tenor whereof ensuethe in form folowinge, that is to say: *[We therefore approve and ratify all these Ordinances, which here follow:]*

Fyrste, that the Taylors within the Cittie of Lichffelde may be allowed for a companye and Brotherhoode of the occupacion of Tailors; and also that none that hathe not bynne Apprentyce within the saide Cittie, be admytted to the saide occupacion to occupie as a master, Iourney-man, or servaunte within the said Cittie, excepte he be sworne vpon the Holie Evangeliste before the wardens of the saide company, to be obedient to the Master and Wardens of the saide occupacion, for the tyme beynge, in all thynges lawfull concernynge the saide occupacion, and the statutes, rules, and ordynances towchynge or concernynge the same, and also dulie and trulie to observe and kepe all these statutes and ordynaunces and euerye of them, vppon payne of forfeytynge for every tyme offendynge the contrarye, iij s iiij d, the one halff thereof to be to the Baylieffes of the saide Cittie, and the other halffe thereof to be to the vse of, and maynteinaunce of, the saide companye / *[1. The Tailors in Lichfield form a Brotherhood, to which no one except Apprentices shall be admitted unless he swears to obey its Rulers and Rules, under a penalty of 3s. 4d.]*

[2] Item, It is ordeyned & agreed by the Master, Warden, and Combretheren of the saide occupacion within the saide Cittie, that no Person or persons shall sette vppe and occupie as a master of the saide occupacion within the said Cittie, that hathe not bynne apprentyce to the same within the saide Cittie, except he ffirste pay, before he open his shoppe-wyndowes, or occupie, or doe openlie any thinge or things towching *[2. No one shall be a Master-Tailor except he has been a City Apprentice,]*

Lichfield Tailors. First Ordinances, 1576.

<small>unless he pays 3s. 4d. to the Wardens at once,

and in a month joins the Brotherhood and pays £4,</small>

or concerning the saide mysterie or crafte, iij s iiij d̃ to the wardens of the said occupacion; and if he occupie there by the space of one monethe, that then he to be sworen Brother to the saide occupacion, and then to paye to the wardens of the saide occupacion iiij li for his Brotherhode; the one halff thereof to be to the Baylieffes and Citezens of the saide Cittie, and the other halff thereof to be to the use and mayntenaunce of the said occupacion; and if he or they will not obeye

<small>under a Penalty of 3s. 4d.</small>

thes statutes and ordynaunces, that then he to paye and forfeyte for euery day he occupyethe after having warnynge by the wardens of the saide occupacion, iijs iiijd̃, to the vses aforesaide.

<small>3. No Apprentice</small>

[3] Item, it is ordeyned and agreed by the ffellowshippe of the saide occupacion, that no person or per-

<small>shall set up as a Master till he pays</small>

sons shall sette vppe and occupie as a master of the saide occupacion within the saide Cittie, that hathe bynne apprentyce there to the same, but that he pay before he open his shoppe-windowes, or occupye or do anythinge or thinges openlye towchinge or concernynge the saide mysterie or crafte, to the master or wardyns

<small>3s. 4d. at once,

and 3s. 4d. more in 2 months.</small>

of the saide occupacion, iij s iiij d̃; and if [he][1] occupie by the space of two moneths, then he to paye for his brotherhoode iij s iiijd̃; the one halffe thereof to be to the Baylieffes and Cytezens of the same Cittie, and the other halffe thereof to the vse of the foresaide occupacion.

<small>4. No Stranger shall work in the City unless</small>

[4] Item, it is ordeyned that no foreygner' beinge of the saide occupacion shall worke in any house or houses within the saide Cittie, wherebie the saide Masters and Bretheren of the saide occupacion shall or may be hyndered of there lyvyng, proffite or commodities,

<small>he takes a shop, as required by 28 Hen. VIII, c. 5.</small>

except he take a shoppe and worke openlie, accordynge to the statutes made in the tyme of kynge Henrie the

---

[1] The omission of the article is regular. See Dr. Kellner's Introduction to *Blanchardyn*.

Eight,[1] vppon payne of forffeytinge for every day offendynge the contrarye, vj s viij d to the vses aforesaide / — Penalty 6s. 8d. a day.

[5] Item, it is ordeyned and agreed that noe Combrother of the saide occupacion shall take any servante to teache hym his occupacion, vnder the Terme of Seven yeres, bounde by Indenture; and that they haue but twoe apprentyces at any one tyme; but that he att any tyme within two yeres, att thend of the last yeres of his former apprentyses, maye take one other to be bounde in forme aforesaide, vppon payne of forfeytinge, every one offendinge the contrary, xl s, the one halffe thereof to be to the Baylieffes and Cytezens of the same Cittie, and the other halffe thereof to the uses of the saide occupacion. — 5. No Brother shall teach any one but a 7-years' Apprentice, or have more than 2 Apprentices, save in the last 2 years of any one's term. Penalty 40s.

[6] Item, it is ordeyned and agreed that if any of the saide occupacion, by the Iudgement of the Wardens of the saide Companye, shall be adiudged to destroy or marre any garment put to hym or them to be made, that then he or they to make recompence for the same to the Owner thereof, at the oversight of the Wardens of the saide occupacion for the tyme beinge, or ells he or they, for offendinge, to forfeyte and pay xl s to the vses aforesaide. — 6. Brethren shall pay for all work they mar. Penalty 40s.

[7] Item, it is ordeyned and agreed that no Master or Combrother of the saide occupacion shall entise, mayntayne, or sette on worke any servaunt or apprentyce that is in Covenaunt with any of his Combretheren without lycense of his saide master, vppon payne of forfaytinge every day, after he hath knowledge or warnynge thereof by his othere master or wardens of the saide occupacion, vi s viiij d, the one — 7. No Brother shall entice away another's Apprentice. Penalty 6s. 8d.

---

[1] See 21 Hen. VIII. c. 16, and 32 Hen. VIII. c. 16, also 5 Eliz. c. 4. See also the Act 14 & 15 Hen. VIII. c. 2, limiting Aliens' Apprentices to two, and putting alien handicraftsmen within two miles of London City under the Gild-Wardens of their Handicrafts. This was made perpetual by 21 Hen. VIII. c. 16. See 28 Hen. VIII. c. 5.

halffe thereof to be to the Baylieffes and Cytezens of the saide Cittye, and the other halffe thereof to be to the vse of the saide occupac*i*on.

8. Brethren shall not be absent from Meetings.

[8] Item, it is ordeyned and agreed that no Master' or Combrother' of the saide occupac*i*on, shall absent hymselffe ffrom his Combretheren when he is lawffully warned by the Wardens of the saide occupac*i*on or there deputies, except he haue a reasonable cause allowed, and approved after by the Master' and Wardens of the saide company, vppon payne of forfaytinge for every tyme offending the Contrary, xij^d, to the vses aforesaide.

Penalty 12d.

9. Apprentices claiming the Freedom of the Brotherhood shall, in their last year,

[9] Item, it is ordeynd and agreed that from henceforth all masters havinge any servaunte or apprentise of the saide occupac*i*on that will clayme any ffredome or pryvyledge w*i*thin this Cittie, by reason of his servyce or prentisshippe, that they the saide servauntes or apprentyces shall resorte within the last Yere of his Terme, and come before the Baylieffes of the said Cittie, and the Masters and Wardyns of the saide occupac*i*on for the tyme beinge, and then and there to be sworen to obey and Keepe all ordynances and Statutes made or vsed conce*r*nynge the saide occupac*i*on, and then and there haue or offer or tender his name entred before the saide Bayelieff*es*, Master, and Wardyns of the saide occupac*i*on, or ells to lose his libe*r*tee and Freedome for ever'.

be sworn to keep the Ordinances.

10. Yearly, within a month of June 24, Midsummer Day, a Master and 2 Wardens shall be chosen,

[10] Item, it is ordeyned and agreed that yerely, w*i*thin one monethe after the feast of the Natyvitie of Saynte Iohn Baptiste, there shalbe a Master' of the saide occupacion and two Wardyns chosen, the saide Master to be chosen contynually by The officers the Yere before, and the Wardyns to be chosen yerely by the consent of the combretheren of the saide occupac*i*on, and they to be officers vntill that day twelve-monethe, and they in there yere shall take payne to

levye and gather' all suche Duties and forfeytures, as shall happen to be dewe in there yere; and also yearlie on the saide day of the saide eleccion shall make a treue accoumpt to the saide Baylieffes of all suche money as they shall haue Received, or be charged withe the receipte of in there yere; and also then and there yelde and paye to the saide Baylieffes, the one halffe of suche forfeytures and somes of money as shall happen to be deue vnto them in that yere past; And also make yerely on the same daye one convenyent and competent Dynner to all the Masters and combretheren) of the saide occupacion; and euery one of them to pay porcion like towarde the charges of the foresaide dynner'; And if any Combrother' be absent att' that tyme, then he or they so beynge absent, to paye like porcion to the Boxe or common-stocke as the Masters pay at there Dinner', vppon payne of forfaytinge for euery tyme offendynge the contrary, iij s iiij d, to be devyded as before is saied / *to levy dues and forfeits,*

account for all monies,

pay half to the City Bailiffs,

and hold a Dinner for the Brethren,

each paying his share.

Penalty 3s. 4d.

[11] Item, it is ordeyned and agreed that yt shalbe lawffull for the Master and Wardens of the saide occupacion, by the assistaunce of the Sergeantes of the saide Cittie for the tyme beynge, for everye somme of money aforesaide, and due by meanes of these ordynaunces, to distrayne; and the distresse so taken) to withholde, vntill suche tyme [as] the summe so fforfeyted be paide. *11. The Master and Wardens may distrain for penalties.*

All whiche Ordynaunces, statutes, Rules and constytucions above mencioned, we the saide Justices, accordinge to the Acte of Parlyament above remembred, and by the auctoryte to vs geven) by the same, doe approbrate, and allowe to be and stande in force and effecte accordynge to the purporte of the same. *These Ordinances, we, the Lord Chief Baron and Justice Lovelace, approve.*

Provided always, that if any ambiguytie, doubt, or questyon shall hereafter happen to arise vppon the takinge, construccion or meanynge of any article, clause *Provided that all questions as to the meaning of the Ordinances* or sentence conteyned in this present Booke, or that any person or persons shall at any tyme hereafter complayne and declare them-selves to the Justices of Assise of this Countie of Stafford for the tyme beinge, that *and all complaints of outsiders* they be vexed or trowbeled in bodie or goodes by reason of these ordynaunces aforsaide, or any of them, otherwise than by the lawes and statutes of this Realme they oughte to be, by the abvsynge, mysinterpretacion or mystakinge of these ordynaunces or any of them, that then, not onlye the same ambyguitye, doubt, or questyon, *shall be settled by the Justices of Assise.* to be ffrom tyme to tyme discussed, reformed and revoked by the saide Justices of Assise, but also all the saide ordynaunces or euery of them, by the discrecion of the saide Justices of Assise, or any of them for the tyme beinge, to be vtterly made frustrate and voyde, as *Given at Stafford, April 6, 1576.* to hym or them shall seeme good. Yeven⁾ at the towne of Stafford in the seid county of Stafford, in our Circuit & progress, the day and yere first above written.

[Signed]
    Edward Saunders [Lord Chief Baron]
    William Lovelace [Sergeant at Law].

[A new Charter for the Lichfield Tailors, dated July 23, 1687, was engrost for execution (and a copy on parchment made of it), but was never executed : it has no seal on the parchment tag prepared for one, and it has no signatures. Nearly ten years later, another Charter, dated May 30, 1697, which is printed below, was duly executed, or signd and seald. It contains 16 Clauses, including almost all the 12 clauses of the proposed Charter of 1687, but differs in certain particulars which are noted in the footnotes to the print of it which follows here.]

SECOND EXTANT CHARTER OF THE LICHFIELD TAILORS.[1]

May 30, 1697.

[2]**To all Christian People** to whom these presents shall come, George Newell, gent*leman*, and Roger Wright, Gent*leman*, the now Bailiffs of the City of Lichfield, and their one and twenty brethren of the corporac*i*on of the said City, Citizens of the said City, send Greeting in our Lord God Everlasting : /.[2]   *The 2 Bailiffs and 21 Brethren of Lichfield Corporation greet you.*

Whereas the Trade of a Taylor within the City and County of the City of Lichfield is, and long hath been, a very laudable and antient trade, and very beneficiall for the educac*i*on of many young persons Inhabiting in and neare the said City; and forasmuch as Stra*u*ngers & Foreigners not haveing served as apprentices within the said City, [3]and others which have not fully served their apprentishippe to the said Trade, have endeavored to sett up the said Trade in the said City, and after some short time have pretended to the like immunityes, priviledges, and Freedoms, as those that have actually served their apprenttishippe in the said City, or purchased their Freedome, & are Denizens or Freemen thereof,[3] By Reason whereof many deceipts, disorders, and irregularityes have Crept in and bin vsed amongst the said Taylors, to the desperagement of their   *As strangers not apprentist in Lichfield have set up as Tailors,*

---

[1] In the margin is a round denoting stamp mark, 'No 8 at 12*d*.' The Revenue stamp of '1 Shilling' is below.

[2–2] The proposed Charter of 1687 was to be from the Mayor and Aldermen, and has not this first paragraph. I don't note every variation of that Charter, but only the chief ones.

[3–3] Not in proposed Charter of 1687.

and so harmd the Tailors who were apprentist in the City,	Trade, discouragement of those who might bee apprentices, and impoverishing of such as have served their apprentishippe in the said City, and are Freemen
the Lichfield Tailors have askt us to make them a Company,	thereof; For Remedy whereof the Taylors within the said City have petitioned us, the said Bailiffs and Citizens of the said City, that they may bee made a Company and Society within the said City, Whereof
with a Master and 2 Wardens,	One to bee nominated and called by the name of the "Master," and two others by the name of "Wardens,"
and to grant them fresh Ordinances.	of the said Company of Taylors, and to Grant vnto them severall by-laws and Ordinances, for the better manageing the said Trade, and Redressing the said
We Bailiffs and Citizens do therefore	Greivances; Now know yee, that wee, the said [1]Bailiffs and Citizens[1] of the said City,—considering the said peticion, and being desirous to regulate and Rectifye the said disorders and irregularityes for the future,—
	Doe (according to the power and autority given unto us by the Charter of our late Soveraigne Lord King [2]Charles the second, and other his Royall progenitors[2]),
grant these Lichfield Tailors the Ordinances following:	by, and with one assent, consent, and agreement, Grant, appoynt, and Make The orders, constitucions, Ordinances, and by-Lawes, herein-after mencioned and contayned, to bee for ever hereafter duly observed & kept by [3]all and every person and persons vseing or ffolloweing the Trade of a Taylor, within the said City and County of Lichfield[3] : /.
1. The Tailors of Lichfield are and shall be	Imprimis, Wee doe Grant, agree, order, and appoynt, That the Tailors within the said City of Lichfield, shall for ever hereafter bee, and are hereby made, a Company and Society within the said City, & called
a Brotherhood or Company.	by the name of "the Maister, Wardens, and Brotherhood of the Company of Taylors," and by that name shall sue & bee sued./

[1]–[1] Mayor and Aldermen, 1687.
[2]–[2] James the Second, 1687.
[3]–[3] the sayd Trade and Company of Taylors. 1687.

Lichfield Tailors. Second Ordinances, 1697.

[2] Item, Wee doe hereby Constitute, Nominate and appoynt Isaack Mat[c]hett to bee The First maister of the said Company, and Thomas Lauder and Thomas Ashmole to be the First Wardens[1] of the said Company, who shall continue in those respective places & offices, vntill the Feast of Saint John Baptist next ensueing; And that Richard Herbert, Thomas Richards, Abraham Taylor [1½ *lines of names scratcht out and markt over*][2] bee of the said Company and Brotherhood; And that the said Company shall & may have and keep a Booke for the Entering of all penaltyes, Fines, Composicions, and Forfeitures, and for the Inrolling the names of all Freemen and apprentices belonging to the said Trade & Company; And that the said Company shall and may receive and take one Moyety, or halfe parte of all paynes, penaltyes, Fines, Forfeitures, and Composicions, to the vse and behoofe of the Bayliffs & Citizens of the said City for the time being (Except as herein-after is Excepted), and the other Moyety or halfe part of the said Fines, Forfeitures, paynes and penaltyes, to the proper vse of the said Company of Taylors, The said Company of Taylors, being assisted by the servants & Officers, of the said Bayliffs and Citizens, and their successers, for the Gathering & Collecting the same.

2. Isaac Matchett is the 1st. Master, and T. Lauder and T. Ashmole the first Wardens, till June 24.

The Company shall have a Book for Fines, and names of Freemen and Apprentices.

Half the Fines, &c., shall go to the City,

and half to the Tailors' Company.

[3] Item, Wee do hereby order,[3] ordeyne and appoynt that noe Foreigner or stranger who hath not

3. No one who hasn't

---

[1] Jonathan Alport, Master of the Company, and Thomas Richards and Isaac Matchett, Wardens. 1687.

[2] The Charter of 1687 says 'William Bond, Samuel Emery, Richard Herbert, Jonathan Alport, Thomas Richard, James Matchett, Michael Lamb, William Sandles, Thomas Hossard, Thomas Mashader, Francis Shaw, Symon Twiford, Charles Gee, Ralph Spencer, Theophilus Bott, Arthur Stanford, Edmund Bond, Abraham Taylor, Samuel Emery junior, Thomas Ashmold, Thomas Parker, Elizabeth Smith, Thomas Bradock, Edward Shaw, & Henry Bond (&) Thomas Launder.'

[3] Parts of the next six lines in the MS. are too worn to be read, and are therefore printed from the copy of it made in 1726.

Lichfield Tailors. Second Ordinances, 1697.

<small>been Apprentice in the City for 7 years may be a Tailor there</small>

been an apprentice by Indenture, or served as an apprentice by the space of Seaven years to the said Trade within the said City, shall vse or exercise the said Trade within the said City, untill hee or they shall have ffirst payd, or secured to bee payd, to the Maister and Warden of the said Company for the time

<small>until he pays the Company £10 for his Freedom,</small>

being, for his or their Freedom to the said Trade, the sume of Tenn Pounds, or otherwise agreed and compounded with the said Master and Wardens, or the Major parte of the said Company, by and with the Consent of the Bayliffs[1] of the said City for the time

<small>and is sworn</small>

being, nor before hee shall bee sworn a Freeman of the said Company within the said City, (in the presence of the Maister and wardens of the said Company, or one of them), before the Bayliffs of the said City, or one of them, and the Towne clerke of the said City or his

<small>and enrold a Freeman of the Company.</small>

sufficient Deputy, and bee inrolled a Freeman of the said Company by the said Towne Clerke or his Deputy, On payne of Forfeiting to the said Maister & Wardens for the time being, to the vses before mencioned, the

<small>Penalty, 40s. a month.</small>

sume of Forty shillings per mensem, for every month any person or persons shall offend in the premises, or act contrary to this Order or Ordinance : /.

<small>4. All who take</small>

[4][2] Item, It is hereby ordered and ordeyned that every person and persons,—as well those that have served their apprentishipps within this City, as those

<small>the Freeman's oath shall swear allegiance to the King,</small>

that purchase or Compound for their Freedome,—shall, in taking the oath of a Freeman, bee sworne to bear Fayth and true allegiance to the King & his lawfull

---

[1] the Mayor. 1687. That Charter omits the next part about being sworn a Freeman : the man is only to be sworn to be obedient to the Major, Master and Wardens (almost as in Article 4, below) 'in all things lawfull concerninge the occupacion or Trade of Taylors, and the good Orders, Rules and Ordinances concerninge the same.' The penalty is 40s. a month, as above.

[2] This Article 4 is not in the proposed Charter of 1687, except as mentioned in the last footnote.

Successors, to bee obedient to the Bayliffs of the said City, and to the Maister and Wardens of the said Company for the time being, in all lawfull things concerning the said trade, and to observe the Orders, Rules and Ordinances made to the Company of Taylors aforesaid, to bear and pay Lott and Scott as other Freemen of the said City, and to defend the said City to the best of their power, For which oath and Inrollment of such Freedome, there shall be payd by each party sworne and Inrolled, Viz^t. To the Bayliffs for the time being, Three shillings Fourepence; To the Town clerke, Three shillings Fourepence; and To the Maister and Wardens of the said Company, Three shillings Fourepence.

[5] Item, Forasmuch as the takeing apprentices for a short time, and the takeing many apprentices by any one person of the said Trade, hath bin found very prejudiciall to the said Trade within the said City, It is therefore hereby ordered, Ordeyned and appoynted, That noe Maister or Freeman of the said Trade within the said City, shall att any time hereafter take any apprentice, or person to serve as an apprentice, for lesse time than Seaven years, wherein noe Fraud shall bee vsed by antedateing the Indenture or articles by which such apprentice shall bee bound, Nor more time than three months allowed for tryall or likeing of such apprentice; And that noe Maister or Freeman of the said Trade now haveing, or which hereafter shall have one apprentice, shall take any other apprentice till Five years bee expired of his First Apprentice time; and soe from time to time shall not take any apprentice oftner than once in Five yeares, (Except where or when it shall happen that any apprentice shall dye, Goe to serve the King, or Run away from his maister, Or bee and continue soe long sick upon his Maisters Lands as that the Maister and Wardens of the said

Lichfield Tailors. Second Ordinances, 1697.

then he may take a Substitute,

Company, or the Major part of them shall agree (if necessary) to allow such Maister another apprentice instead of such Sicke, dead or Runaway apprentice, to preserve his said Maisters Custome and Trade: In which case only, such Freeman or Maister may take another apprentice), Caution & notice thereof being First given by such Maister or Freeman to the Maister & Wardens of the said Company for the time being, of the departure & losse of such apprentice from his

If the Company approve.

service; And the same being approved by the Maister, Wardens and Company, or the Major part of them, that the same was not occasioned, contrived, Feigned or Consented unto by such Freeman or Maister, On payne of Forfeiting to the Maister and Wardens of the said Company, to the vses aforesaid, for every offence against this Ordinance or any Clause of it, Five Pounds : /.[1]

6. Every Apprentice's name shall be enterd within a month in the Company's Book.

[6] Item, It is hereby Ordered, Ordeyned and appoynted, That every Maister or Freeman that shall take any apprentice, shall, within One month after hee shall soe take or receive such apprentice, Enter the name of such apprentice with the Maister & wardens for the time being, On payne of Forfeiting to the said Maister and Wardens for the time being, to the vses

Penalty 3s. 4d. à month.

aforesaid, the summe of Three shillings Foure pence for every month he shall neglect soe doeing; for which Entrance, there shall bee payd to the Maister & War-

Fee, 2s. 6d.

dens for the time being, Two shillings Six pence /.

7. No Apprentice

[7] Item, It is hereby Ordeyned, appoynted and agreed, that noe person or persons (although hee or they shall have served an apprenticeshipp to the said

shall set up as

trade within the said City) shall sett up or doe any

---

[1] For this Article 5, the proposed Charter of 1687 has an Article 4, that no Master or Freeman shall take more than one Apprentice for 7 years; but that when 5 years of this time are expired, he may take another Apprentice for 7 years.

act or thing openly touching or concerning the said Mistery or trade of a Taylor, as a Maister thereof, or shall bee sworne or admitted a Freeman of the said Trade, before hee or they shall have Compounded with the Maister & Wardens for the time being, for his or their Freedome, and shall have actually paid to such Maister & Wardens such summe of money (not exceeding Twenty shillings, nor lesse than Six shillings Eight pence) as shall be sett and appoynted by such Maister & Wardens, and Major part of the said Company;[1] The one Moyety whereof shall bee to the vse of the said Bayliffs and Citizens & their Successors, and the other Moyety to the vse of the said Company : /. *a Tailor in Lichfield till he's compounded for his Freedom, and paid from 6s. 8d. to 20s.*

[8] Item, It is Ordered, Ordeyned and appointed, that noe Maister or Combrother of the said Company, shall entice away, imploy, entertaine, sett on worke, the servant, Journeyman, or apprentice, of any of his Combrethren, without the Licence of the Maister of such servant, Journeyman or apprentice, with whom hee or they last worked, upon payne of fforfeiting to the Maister and Wardens for the time being, to the vses aforesaid, for every day after Notice given by the Maister from whom Such Servant, Journeyman, or apprentice shall soe depart, or by the Wardens of the said Company for the time being, or any of them, unto the said Maister that shall soe entice away, imploy, Entertaine, or sett on worke any such Servant, Journeyman or apprentice, that shall (as aforsaid) Leave his Maister, the summe of six shillings Eightpence : /. *8. No Master or Brother shall entice away another's Apprentice. Penalty 6s. 8d. a day.*

[9] Item, It is Ordered, ordeyned and appoynted That if any Maister or freeman of the said Trade, or Combrother, haveing Reasonable notice and warning *9. No Freeman shall be absent from Company Meetings.*

---

[1] The Charter of 1687 makes 3s. 4d. payable before the person settling up as a Tailor does ' anything openly touching or conceringe the said Mystery or Craft,' and another 3s. 4d. ' if he occupy for the space of two Months.'—Article 5.

Lichfield Tailors. Second Ordinances, 1697.

of any Meeting to bee appoynted by the Maister & Wardens of the said Company for the time being, shall, without reasonable excuse (to bee allowed and approved by the Maister and Wardens), absent himself from such meeting, such person soe absenting shall, for every such default or absence, forfeit & pay, to the vse of the Company of Taylors only, Two Shillings Sixpence : /.[1]

Penalty, 2s. 6d.

10. All who claim the Freedom of the Trade in Lichfield shall first enroll their names in the Company's Book,

[10] Item, It is hereby ordered, ordeyned, and agreed that every person or persons who shall claime any Freedome or priviledge of the said Trade within the said City, doe ffirst Inroll his or their name or names with the Maister & Wardens of the said Company for the time being, for which he shall pay the summe of Three shillings Fourpence; And in case hee shall neglect soe doeing, then hee or they soe neglecting, shall forfeit the summe of Three shillings Fourepence for every month hee or they shall neglect soe doeing,—after Notice thereof given by the said Maister and Wardens,—to the vse of the said Company of Tailors only : /.

and pay 3s. 4d.

Penalty, 3s. 4d. a month.

11. No Freeman shall take a Stranger

[11] Item, It is alsoe Ordered, Ordeyned, and appoynted that noe Maister or Freeman of the said trade within the said City, shall take any Foreigner, Stranger or others not being free of the said Company, or haveing served as an apprentice within the said City by the space of Seaven Yeares, to be his or their Partner or Partners, or otherwise to worke than only as a Journeyman in the said trade, upon payne of fforfeiting to the said Maister & Wardens of the said Company for the time being, for every weeke after notice thereof given by the Maister & Wardens, or any of them, Thirteen shillings Foure pence; one moyety thereof to the vse of the Bayliffs of the said City for

as partner.

Penalty, 13s. 4d. a week.

---

[1] twelvepence, 1687.

Lichfield Tailors. Second Ordinances, 1697.

the time being, and the other Moyety to the vse of the said Company of Taylors : /.

[12] ¹Item, It is Ordered, Ordeyned, and appoynted and agreed, that yearly and every yeare for ever hereafter, upon *the* Feast of the Nativity of St. John Baptist, or within one moneth after, there shall bee a succeeding Master and Wardens chosen out of the said Company, for *the* year next ensueing, which Master shall be chosen by the Wardens for the time being (but in default of their Eleccion, then by the said Company or the Major part of them); And the two Wardens shall be chosen by the Company or the major part of them; And that the said Master & Wardens shall take care for, & cause the Collecting and receiveing of all such forfeitures, paynes & penaltyes as shall happen within their Respective Years, and shall make a true accompt thereof to the Bayliffs of the City for the time being, And to the said Company of Taylors, upon the day of the Eleccion of such new Master and Wardens yearly, and shall then pay and deliver up unto the Bayliffs of the said City for the time being, One Moyety of the Fines, Forfeitures, penaltyes, Composicions, & other moneys as shall bee become due, forfeited, or payable to the said Bayliffs and Citizens of the said City for the time being, and the said Company of Taylors ;² And the other Moyety they shall then likewise (or within Ten days after) pay and deliver up to the next Succeeding Master and Wardens, together alsoe with all such other moneys as shall bee due to the said Company, or remaine in their hands, in the Foot of their accompts, upon payne that each person makeing default or False accompts shall

12. Yearly, on 24 June,

or a month after,

the 2 Wardens shall elect a Master,

and the Company shall elect 2 Wardens,

to see to the Penalties, &c.,

and account for them,

and pay one half of them to the City Bailiffs,

and the other half to the next Master and Wardens.

---

¹ Second or small skin of the Charter : circular denoting stamp 'No. 2 at 5d.' Revenue stamp '1 Shilling.'

² 'All such forfeitures' go to the Master and Wardens under the proposed Charter of 1687.—Article 10.

Lichfield Tailors. Second Ordinances, 1697.

Penalty, &c.

Respectively forfeit to the Bayliffs and Citizens of the said City the sum*m*e of Five Pounds; whereof One Moyety shall be to the vse of the said Bayliffs and Citizens, And the other Moyety to the vse of the said Company of Taylors.

13. The Tailors' Company shall have a Box with 3 keys,

[13] Item, It is hereby ordered, & ordeyned[1] & agreed, that there shall bee provided a Box, with three Locks and three Keys, for the vse of the [2] said Company, which Box, and one of the said Keys, shall bee

of which the Master and Wardens shall keep one each.

kept by the Master of the said Company for the time being, and the other two Keys by the Wardens of the said Company for the time being; and in Case the Master and Wardens, or any of them, shall happen to dye, or bee Removed within that year wherein they shall soe bee Master and Wardens, That they the said Company, or the Major part of them, shall elect a new Master, Warden or Wardens, instead of him or them soe dying or being removed, Which new Master & Warden or Wardens soe of new to bee Elected, shall continue & bee in *th*e office or places to which hee or they shall bee soe elected, vntill the next publick day of Elecc*i*on of Master and Wardens of y*e* said Com-

The Company shall also have a Beadle.

pany; And that the said Company shall & may elect and have One fitt person to attend them, who shall be called by the name of their 'Beadle': /.

14. The Company shall hold 3 Meetings a year,

[14][3] Item, It is ordered, ordeyned and appoynted, that the Master & Wardens of the said Company shall yearly and every year hereafter, appoint and Cause

besides that for electing a Master and Wardens.

three Meetings besides that for the Elecc*i*on of Master & Wardens yearly, to concert[1] the matters and interest of the said trade; One of which meetings shall bee w*i*thin 14 dayes after Mich*a*el*m*as,[1] one other w*i*thin Fourteen dayes after Christmas, and the third Within fourteen days after Lady day, On payn that the Master

---

[1] ? MS.   [2] Col. 2 of second Skin.
[3] This Article is not in the proposed Charter of 1687.

Lichfield Tailors. Second Ordinances, 1697.

and Wardens soe neglecting to appoynt such meetings shall, for every default, Forfeit Twenty shillings a-piece, to the vses of the said Bayliffs, Citizens, & Company of Taylors. *Penalty on not calling such Meetings 20s.*

[15] Item, It is hereby alsoe ordered, ordeyned and agreed, that it shall and may bee lawfull to and for the Master & Wardens of the said Company for the time being,—with the Assistance of the Serjeants att Mace of the said City for the time being (as the Charter of *the* said City doth in that behalfe impower),—to demand, collect & gather all such Fines, Forfeitures and penaltyes as shall bee forfeited by any person or persons whomsoever, offending against the Orders, Ordynances, and appoyntments aforesaid, and upon refusall of payment, to Destreyne for the same; And the Distress or Distresses soe to bee had or taken, to keepe and detayne vntill such Forfeitures, Fines and penaltyes, together with the charges thereby occasioned, bee fully payd and satisfyed : /. *15. The Master and Wardens (assisted by the City Serjeant) shall collect the Company's fines and penalties, and distrain for the same.*

[16] Item, it is hereby ordered, ordeyned, and agreed that the Master & Wardens for the time being, & such and soe many of the Brotherhood as the Master and Wardens shall direct, shall be attending upon the Bayliffs[1] of the *said* City for *th*e time being, on Sondays, to the Chappell & Cathedrall Church, & other publick meetings, as the Bayliffs for the time being shall require, On payne that every One neglecting such meeting without reasonable excuse, shall forfeit Twelvepence each time, to the uses aforesa*id*. In Witnesse whereof, Wee the said [2]Bayliffs, and One and Twenty Brethren, have att a Comon Hall hereto[2] affixed our Comon Seal, the Third day of May, in the Ninth Yeare of the Raign of Our Soveraigne Lord, William *16. The Officers and Brotherhood shall attend the Bailiffs at Sunday Cathedral Services, &c. Penalty, 12d. Common Seal of the City of Lichfield affixt,*

---

[1] Major. 1687.
[2-2] Major and Aldermen have hereunto 1687.

3 May, 1697. the Third,¹ by the Grace of God, of England, Scotland, France and Ireland, King, defender of the Fayth, &c, Anno Domini 1697 : /.

[Signd] Geo Newell.   Roger Wright.
Bayliffs.²

¹ the five and twentith day of July in the third year of the Raigne of our Soveraigne Lord, James the Second.   1687.
² The copy has at its end: "Concordat hæc Copia cum Originali. Exam*inatu*m decimo Novembri, Anno D*omi*ni 1726."

FIRST EXTANT ORDINANCES OF THE LICHFIELD SMITHS' GILD.

3 Aug. 1601.

To all Christian people to whome this present wryting shall come, greeting in our Lord God everlasting!

Knowe yee that whereas peace preserveth and maketh comon-wealthes to flouryshe, and discorde decayeth and distroyeth the same, And there can be no peace where there are noe lawes to releyve and reward the honest and vertuous, and to correct and chastice the wicked and reprobate, And whereas at the parliament holden at westmynster, the fyve and twentith daye of Ianuarie, in the nynetenth yeare of the Raigne of the laite kynge of famous memorye, Henrye the Seaventh, yt was enacted that noe maysters, wardens, and fellowshippes of Craftes or mysteryes, or any of theym, nor any rulers of Guildes or Fraternyties should take vpon theym to make any actes or ordynances, ne to execute any actes or ordynances by theym theretofore made in disheritance or dymynucion of the prerogatyue of the kyng, nor of other, nor agaynst the common proffytt of the people, but if the same actes or ordinances be examyned and approved by the Chancellour, Treasorer of England, or cheife Iustice, of eyther benche, or three of theym, or bifore both the Iustices of Assises in their Cyrcuyt or progresse in the Shire where such actes or ordynances be made, vpon payne of forfiture of fortie poundes for every tyme that they doe the con-

As Peace makes Commonwealths flourish,

and cannot exist without good Laws,

and as Parliament in 1503

enacted that no Crafts should thenceforth make

any Ordinances

save with the approval of Two Judges of Assise,

Lichfield Smiths. First Ordinances, 1601.

the Smiths and like trades

trary. **Nowe** the Mayster, wardens and fellowship of the Craftes & mysteries of Smythes, goldsmythes, Iron-mongers, Cardmakers, Pewtereres, Plumbers, Cutlers

of Lichfield

& Spurryers in the Cyttie of Lychfeild, being an auncient Societie of Mayster, two wardens, & Fellowship of the mysteries aforesaid, according to the said act of parlia-

have askt us, Justices Walmysley and Warburton,

ment haue made humble peticion vnto Thomas Walmysley and Peter Warburton, two of her maiesties Iustices of the common Benche, & Iustices of Assyse, as well in the County of Stafford (within which countie the said Cyttye of Lychfeild hath auncientlye been) as in the countie of the said Cyttie of Lychfeild, that it

to approve their Ordinances here following:

would please theym to examyne & approve the actes & ordinances hearunder wrytten, being some of theym auncient, & some of theym newe and latelie set downe, before the same should haue the name, or be published or sett forthe as any actes or ordinances, that vnder their approbacion the state of the said Craftes & mysteries in the said Cyttie might be prosperous, and their common welthe florishe:—

1. Every year,

[1] **Imprimis**,—according to the commendable custome vsed as well in the said Cyttie as in other Cytties and townes within this Realme of England, that the governours of corporacions, fellowships and Societies are yearlie changed, and new chosen in their places, It is nowe, therefore,—by the Mayster & two wardens and fellowship of the said craftes and mysteries within the said Cyttye of Lychfeild—ordeyned, & ordered that

on the Friday after Nov. 23,

there shalbe yearlie, on frydaye next after the feast day of St. Clement, a metinge at some place convenyent within the said Cyttie, by the Mayster & wardens & thothers of the bretheren of the said Societie or fellow-

the Brethren shall meet,

shipp, or the greater nomber of theym, betwene the howers, of eight & eleuen of the clocke in the aforenoone of the same day, where the greater nomber of theym so meetinge togeather shall & may procede to

Lichfield Smiths. First Ordinances, 1601.

the newe eleccion of a newe maister & wardens; & when their eleccion is so made, the maister & wardens so chosen & made, shall contynue Maister & wardens of the said fellowship for that one yeare following, & vntill a new Maister & wardens be chosen as aforesaid, if the same be made within fowertene dayes next after the ende of the said yeare. Neuertheles, if eyther the Maister or wardens for the tyme being, or any of theym, shall dye within the yeare, or departe from the said Cittie & dwell elswhere, then the bretheren of the said societie shall, in euerye such case as occasion serveth, call a new assemblie at some convenient place within the said Cyttie, & procede to a newe eleccion in maner & forme aforesaid, to supplie euery such defect, & to contynue out the remnant of the yeare in which such defect happeneth. And if any, being a freman of the said Craftes & Mysteries within the same Cyttie, shall— after notice gyven or sent vnto him of the tyme & place by the Maister of the said Craftes & Mysteries for the tyme being—willinglie or without reasonable excuse absent himself, & not be present at euery such eleccion within the said Cyttie, that then euery of theym so being absent shall forfett vnto the Maister, Wardens & fellowship of the said Craftes & Mysteries for the tyme being, six shillinges, eight pence, wherof the moytie shalbe to their common box, & thother moytie to the poore people within the said Cyttie, to be distributed at the discrecion of the maister & wardens for the tyme being.

[2] **Item**, it is further ordeyned by the said Maister, wardens & fellowship, that none of theym shall at any tyme take any apprentice or covenaunt-servant for shorter tearme then seaven yeares, & that within the yeare after the retayner of any such servant, aswell the proper name & sirename of the maister as of such servant, & the nomber of yeares to be by him served,

and elect a new Master and 2 Wardens

to continue for a year, and till their successors are chosen.

But if any die,

substitutes shall be elected at a new Meeting.

Any Freeman

not present at an Election shall

be fined 6s. 8d.

2. No apprentice shall be taken

for less than 7 years.

togeather with the facultie in which he is to be trayned vp, shalbe by the maister & servant inrolled or put in writing in a booke of the said Craftes & mysteries, which shall from tyme to tyme remayne with the senior of the two wardens for the tyme being.

3. No man shall carry on a trade of the Company

[3] **Item**, it is ordeyned & established by the said Maister, wardens & fellowship, that no man shall hearafter sett vp & exercyse his occupacion in any of the said Craftes or mysteryes within the said Cyttie (except such as haue bene apprentice in the same Cittie according to the ordynaunce next before) other then such as

unless he has paid and been admitted to it.

shall first agree with the maister & wardens of the said Craftes or Mysteries for the tyme being, & be admytted & allowed by theym, vpon payne to forfeyt for euery

Penalty 6s. 8d.

such offence six shillinges eight pence, the moitie whereof shalbe to the Common box, & thother moitie to the poore people within the said Cittie, to be distributed at the discrecion of the Maister & wardens for the tyme being.

4. Seven-year Apprentices shall

[4] **Item**, that euery one which haith, or hearafter shall haue served any apprentyship in any of the said Craftes or mysteries within the said Cittie for the space of seaven yeares, or for any longer tearme, shalbe by

be made free of the Company by their masters

his Maister made free of the same mysterye, if the said servant be desirous soe to be, & be admytted & allowed as aforesaid, & will pay to the Maister, wardens and fellowship of the same Craftes and mysteries within

on paying 6s. 8d.

the said Cittie for the tyme being, six shillinges eight pence; vpon payne that euery maister[1] offending against this ordinaunce shall forfayt to the Maister, wardens &

Penalty 20s.

Fellowship of the said craftes or mysteries, twenty shillinges; the moitie of which penaltie shalbe to the Common box, & thother moitie therof to the poore people of the said Cittie, to be distributed at the discrecion of the Maister & wardens for the tyme being.

[1] That is, Master of an apprentice.

[5] **Item**, that no person of any of the said Craftes or misteries not hauing bene apprentice within the said Cittie as aforesaid, shall set vp or exercise any of the said Craftes or mysteries within the said Cittie, vnles he be first admitted & sworne a brother of the said fellowship, & pay for the same vnto the maister & wardens for the tyme being, tenn poundes; vpon payn to forfeyt vnto the maister, wardens & Fellowship of the said Craftes or mysteries, for euery offence against this ordinance, tenn poundes; wherof the moytie shalbe to their common box, & thother moytie to the poore people of the said Cittie, to be distributed at the discrecion of the maister & wardens for [the] tyme being.

5. No one save an Apprentice shall carry on a Company-trade till he is admitted

and pays £10.

Penalty £10.

[6] **Item**, it is ordeyned that no maister or brother of any of the said Craftes or mysteryes within the said Cittie shall intyce, hier, or take to worke, any Iourneyman, prentice, or servant of any brother or maister of the said Craftes or mysteries, without the licence & consent of his maister, vpon payne to forfeyt to the said maister, wardens & fellowship, for euery such offence, tenn shillinges, wherof the moytie shalbe to their comon box, and thother moytie to the poore people of the said Cyttie, to be distributed at the discrecion of the maister & wardens for the tyme being.

6. No Brother shall employ another's workman

without consent.

Penalty 10s.

[7] **Item**', it is ordeyned that no maister or brother of the said Craftes or mysteries hearafter shall suffer any forrenner or other—except such as are his apprentizes—to worke in his shoppe, or house, or elsewhere within the said Cittie, for him, or for any other by his meanes, without the licence of the maister & wardens of the said craftes & mysteryes in the said Cyttie for the tyme being, vpon payne to forfeyt for euery such offence, vnto the said maister, wardens & fellowship, thre shillinges and fower pence, to be put into their comon box.

7. No Brother shall let any Stranger work for him without license from the Master and Wardens.

Penalty 3s. 4d.

[8] **Item**', that no maister or brother of the said

8. No Master-

GILDS. E

Smith shall shoe a horse that another Brother has pared.

mysterye of Smythes w*i*thin the said Cittie, nor anie of their servant*es*, shall hearafter shoe any horse w*hich* any of his brethren of the said Cyttie hath pared, except there be verie reasonable cause—& the same cause to be allowed by the m*aister* & wardens for the tyme being,—vpon payne to forfeyt for eu*er*y such offence, to the said m*aister*, wardens & fellowship,

Penalty 3s. 4d.

three shilling*es* fower pence ; wherof the moytie shalbe to their com*m*on box, & thother moitie to the poore people of the said Cittie, to be distributed at the discrec*i*on of the m*aister* & wardens for the tyme being.

9. Strangers shall not hawk in Lichfield,

[9] **Item**, it is ordeyned that no forener exercysing any of the said craft*es* or mysteries hearafter, shall haucke w*i*thin the said Cittie, but onelie take a stand-

but only stand in the market or fair.

ing on the markett daye or fayer tyme, vpon payn to forfeyt for eu*er*y such offence, to the said m*aister*,

Penalty 6s. 8d.

wardens & fellowship, six shilling*es* eight pence ; the moytie wherof to be to their comon box, & thother moitie to the poore people of the said Citty, to be distributed at the discrec*i*on of the m*aister* & wardens for the tyme being.

10. No Smith shall go to an inn or house unless he's sent for,

[10] **Item**), that none of the trade of Smythes w*i*thin the said Cittie shall goe to anie of the Innes or Houses w*i*thin the said Cyttie, or send any of his servant*es* to doe any thing belonging to the same trade,

nor shall he bribe servants to get custom.

except he be called or sent for ; neyther shall any of theym gyue rewardes, ould fees, or money to the servant*es* of any of the said Innes or Howses, or any other p*er*son, to haue the Custome of the said house, vpon payne to forfeyt to the m*aister*, wardens & fellowship of the said Craft*es* & mysteries, for eu*er*y such

Penalty 6s. 8d.

offence, six shilling*es* eight pence ; wherof the moytie shalbe to their com*m*on box, & thother moytie to the poore people of the said Cyttie, to be distributed at the discrec*ion*) of the m*aister* & wardens for the tyme being.

[11] **Item,** that no m*aist*er or brother of any of the said craft*es* or mysteries w*i*thin the said Cittie shall hearafter disclose anie councell or commu*n*ycac*i*on concernyng any of their said sciences had at their com*m*on assemblies, neyther make anie brawles, chidyng or contenc*i*on, nor raise or report any false, slanderous, or evill speach or tayle of any of the freemen of any of the said Craft*es* or mysteries within the said Cittie, vpon payne to forfeyt to the m*aiste*r, wardens & fellowship aforesaid, for eue*r*y offence against any part of this ordynaunce, ten shilling*es*; wherof the moitie to be to their com*m*on box, & thother moitie to the poore people of the said Cittie, to be distributed at the discrec*i*on of the m*aiste*r & wardens for the tyme being. *11. No brother shall disclose trade-secrets, or brawl, chide, or slander any Freeman. Penalty 10s.*

[12] **Item,** it is ordeyned that no forener vsing any of the said Craft*es* or mysteries shall take any worke out of the said Cittie belonging to any of the said Craft*es* or mysteries, vpon payne to forfeyt to the m*aiste*r, wardens & fellowship aforsaid, for eue*r*y breach of this ordynance, ten shilling*es*, vnles the m*aiste*r & Wardens first giue consent so to do; wherof the moitie shalbe to their com*m*on box, & thother moytie to poore people of the said Cyttie, to be distributed at the discrec*i*on of the m*aiste*r & wardens for the tyme being. *12. No Stranger shall take any Company work out of the City. Penalty 10s.*

[13] **Item,** that eue*r*y yeare when newe m*aiste*r & wardens of the said Craft*es* or mysteries w*i*thin the said Cyttie shalbe chosen, according to the true meaning of this p*r*esent ordinanc*es*, then there shalbe made by the m*aiste*r & wardens for the yeare next before, to the then newe m*aiste*r, wardens and Fellowship, a true accompt of all such somes of money as they or any of theym haue receyued for the same next yeare preceding, & then pay what shall appeare to be due, vpon payne that eue*r*y one offending against this ordynance, for eue*r*y such offence shall forfeyt to the said newe m*aiste*r, wardens & fellowship, fortie shilling*es*, the *13. On the election of a new Master and Wardens, the outgoing ones shall account to them for all money receivd in the previous year. Penalty 40s.*

E 2

moytie wherof shalbe to their common box, & thother moitie to the poore people of the said Cittie, to be distributed at the discrecion of the maister & wardens for the tyme being.

14. All disputes between Freemen

[14] **Item**, it is ordeyned & established, that if anie dissencion, debate or discord, shall happen betwene any of the free men of the said trades or mysteries within the same Cyttie, that the maister & wardens of the said trades or mysteries within the said Cyttie for the tyme being, may call the parties before theym, & heare & determyne the matter according to right & conscience, before any suyt of lawe be attempted, so that peace may be had emongst theym; vpon payne that euery partie refusing to abyde such hearing & determynyng the controuersie betwene him & theym, or his or their aduersarie or aduersaries, shall forfeyt for euery such his or their refusall, to the maister, wardens & fellowship aforesaid, twentie shillinges, wherof the moytie to be to their common box, & thother moytie to the poore people of the said Cyttie, to be distributed at the discrecion of the maister & Wardens for the tyme being.

shall be heard by the Master and Wardens

before the parties go to law.

Penalty 20s.

15. No Journeyman shall work in his own house.

[15] **Item**, it is ordeyned that noe Iorneyman of any of the said Craftes or mysteries within the said Cyttie shall hearafter worke in his owne house any thing apperteyning to any of the said trades or mysteries, vpon payne to forfeyt to the said maister, wardens & fellowship, for euery such offence, three shillinges fower pence, wherof the moitie to be to their Common box, & thother moytie to the] poore people of the said Cyttie, to be distributed at the discrecion of the maister & wardens for the tyme being.

Penalty 3s. 4d.

16. No Stranger shall sell any wares in the City

[16] **Item**, it is ordeyned that noe forener vsing any of the said Craftes or mysteries shall occupie any standing, or vtter any Wares, within the said Cyttie, belonging to any of the said Craftes or mysteries, but onelie on the markett dayes, fayre tyme, & tyme of

save on Marketdays and at Fairs

markett, viz., betwixt nyne of the clocke in the morning, & fower of the clocke in the after-noone, of any such merkett or fayer day, vpon payne to forfeyt for euery such offence, vnto the maister, wardens & fellowship of the said Craftes & misteries within the said Cittie, fortie shillinges. *(from 9 a.m. to 4 p.m. Penalty 40s.)*

[17] **Item**, it is ordeyned that no person vsing any of the said Craftes or mysteries shall hearafter occupie or cause ¹to be occupied any other of the said craftes or mysteryes within the said Cyttie, but that wherein he haith beene brought vp as an apprentice, according to the true intent of these ordynaunces, vpon payne to forfeyt to the Maister, Wardens & fellowshipp aforesaid, for euery month for offending, twentie shillinges. *(17. Freemen sha'n't practise any trade but the one they were apprentist to. Penalty 20s.)*

[18] **Item**, that none of any of the said Craftes or Mysteries within the said Cyttie shall hearafter buy or cause to be bought any Ware or Wares which any of the freemen of the said trades, craftes or mysteries within the said Cyttye haith bargayned, agreed for, or gyuen earnest for, haveing notyce of the same, vpon payne to forfeyt to the Maister, wardens and fellowship aforesaid, ten shillinges, wherof the moytie to be to their comon box, and thother moytie to the poore people of the said Cyttie, to be distributed at the discrecion of the maister and Wardens for the tyme being. *(18. No Freeman shall buy any wares that another has bargaind for. Penalty 10s.)*

[19] **Item**, if any Maister die, any of his apprentizes not hauing served out the tyme of his apprentiship, in any of the said Craftes or misteries within the said Cyttie, then shall he, within convenyent tyme after request, be placed with some other Maister within the said Cyttie, vntill he haue served out the resydew of the full tyme of his apprentiship, if he intend to be free within the said Cittye of any of the said Craftes or mysteries, & shall soe imploy him- *(19. Apprentices of a Master dying shall either serve the rest of their time with another Master,)*

---

¹ Second skin of parchment.

selfe as he shall not onelie doe his endevour to be sufficient in his art and science, but also doe service to the wydowe of his deceased Maister, by discrecion of the Maister & Wardens of the said craftes & mysteries within the said Cyttie for the tyme being, or els agre with the said Maister and Wardens of the said Craftes or mysteries within the said Cyttye for the tyme being, to thuse of his laite maisteres wydowe, & so depart without his freedome if he be so disposed; vpon payne to forfeyt for euery breach of this ordynance, to the mayster, wardens & fellowship of the said Craftes or mysteries within the said Cyttie, fyve poundes.

[marginal notes: for the benefit of his dead Master's widow, or compound with the Master and Wardens on her behalf, and then leave. Penalty £5.]

[20] **Item,** it is ordeined & established, noe platte of silver, gould or gylt, whole or broken, or any maner of pretious stones or Iewells, or any lattyn, brasse, pewther, or other mettall whatsoeuer, belonging to the trade, craft, or mysterie of goldsmythes or pewterers, whole or broken, shall be bought by any of thinhabitantes of the said Cyttie, or any other vsing any of the trades or mysteries before mencioned, to be sould agayne, or shalbe offered to be sould agayne, vnles it be by any of the goldsmythes or pewtherers within the said Cyttie allowed & made free as aforesaid; vpon payne that euery one so offending, for euerye breach of this ordynance shall forfeyt to the Maister & Wardens of the said Craftes or mysteries within the said Cyttie for the tyme being, ten shillinges: And this ordynance is not to be taken to make lawfull that any goldsmythes should meddle in the trade of pewtherers, nor any pewtherer with the trade of goldsmythes within the said Cyttie.

[marginal notes: 20. No plate, jewels or metal used by goldsmiths or pewterers shall be bought by Lichfield folk for sale again, unless by leave of a Freeman. Penalty 10s.]

[21] **Item,** it is ordeyned & established that none of the said craftes or mysteries within the said Cyttie, nor any other not being free of any of the said trades, craftes or mysteries within the said Cyttye, shall vtter any wares, being wares belonging to any of the said trades, craftes or misteries within the said Cytty, but such as

[marginal notes: 21. Wares of any trade shall be sold only by Freemen]

perteyne to his trade, science, craft or mysterye wherein he haith bene trayned vp, allowed & made free of, within the said Cyttye, And that the same wares perteyning to his trade shalbe vttered in open market or fayer, or in his shopp, & not otherwise, vpon payne to forfeyt to the master, Wardens & fellowship of the said craftes & mysteries, for euery such offence, six shillinges eight pence; wherof thone moytie shalbe to the Comon box, & thother moitie to the poore people of the said Cyttie, to be distributed at the discrecion of the Maister & Wardens of the said Craftes & mysteries for the tyme being.

traind to that trade in Lichfield,

and then only in market, fair, or shop.

Penalty 6s. 8d.

[22] **Item**, if any being free of any of the said trades within the said Cyttye, offend in any thing against any of thordinances in these presentes conteyned, & pay not the penaltie & forfeyture to the maister & wardens for the tyme being, within thirtie dayes after the same forfyture publicklie declared in the Guyldhall of the same Cyttie vpon any thursday in the tyme that the Court of Record within the same Cyttie shall or should be kept, after request by the comon Serieant made to thoffendour & refusall made by thoffendour to pay the same forfeyture, & the same signified to the maister & Wardens by the same Comon serieant in wryting vnder his hand, then euery such offendour shall—in the said open hall, & in the tyme of the said Court-keping—be openlie declared to be disfranchised, And to be neuertheles remytted vpon such redempcion & in such sort as shall seeme good to the maisters & wardens for the tyme being. **All** which statutes, lawes, ordynances & constitucions are ordeyned by the Mayster, Wardens & fellowship of the said Craftes or mysteries in the said Cyttie, to take place & stand in strength & power as statutes & ordynances from such tyme as the said Iustices of Assise shall make Approbacion and allowance therof.

22. Any Freeman breaking any Ordinance,

and not paying the penalty within 30 days,

shall be disfranchised, but may afterwards compromise.

Lichfield Smiths. First Ordinances, 1601.

> All these Ordinances, we two Justices of Assise approve.

All w*h*ich ordynance*s*, statutes and constitucio*n*, we the said Iustices, according to the act of parliament aboue remembred, and by the aucthoritie to vs gyven bye the same, doe approbate and allowe to be and stand in force and effect according to the purport of the same. **Provided** alwayes, that yf any ambiguytie, doubt

> Provided that if any doubts arise on these Ordinances,

or question shall happen to aryse hearafter, vpon the takyng, construccio*n* or meaning of any article therof, or sentence conteyned in this p*re*sent booke, or that any pe*r*son or pe*r*sons shall at any tyme hearafter complayne & declare theymselues to the Iustice*s* of Assise of

> or any one is harmd by them,

this Countie of Stafforde for the tyme being, that they be charged or troubled in bodie or good*es* by reason of these ordynance*s* aforsaid, or any of theym (otherwise then by the lawes & statutes of this Realme he or they ought to be) by thabusing, mystaking or mysinterp*re*tacio*n* of these ordynance*s* or any of theym, or if yt shall happen any myscheife or inconuenyence hearafter to fall out by reason of these ordynances or any of theym, & that the same shall so appeare to & before

> the Justices for the time being may amend

the said Iustice*s* for the tyme being, That then, not onelie the same ambiguyties, myscheife*s*, doubt*es*, questions & inconuenyences to be from tyme to tyme discussed, reformed and corrected by the said Iustice[s] of Assise for the tyme being, but also all the said ordynance*s* and eue*r*y of theym, or soe many of theym as shalbe by the said Iustice*s* in their wisdome, thought

> and reform the same

fytt to be reformed or corrected by the discrecio*n* of the said Iustices of Assise for the tyme being to be vtterlie made frustrate & voyde, or corrected or amended in such sort as by the said Iustice*s* for the tyme being

> by writing signd by them.

shalbe declared, lymyted, or appoynted in wryting subscrybed w*i*th their names. **Geuen** at the towne of

> Given at Stafford 3 Aug., 1601.

Stafford in the Countie of Staff*ord* at the Assises in o*u*r Circuyt, the third day of August in the three and fortith yeare of the raigne of o*u*r soue*r*aigne Ladie

Elizabeth, by the grace of God, Quene of England, France & Ireland, defendo*ur* of the faith, &c.

[Signed]   Tho Walmysley.   P. Warburton.

[Endorst in a later hand] Blacksmiths Company.
3rd August, 43 Eliz., 1601.

SECOND SET OF ORDINANCES OF THE COMPANY OF LICHFIELD SMITHS.

24 July, 1630.

To all Christian People vnto whome this present writinge shall come, William Throppe and Richard Draffgate, the now Bayliffes of the Cittie of Lichfeild, and the One and Twenty Bretheren of the Incorporacion of the said Cittie, send greetinge in our Lord God everlastinge. **Know You** that whereas peace preserveth and maketh Common Wealthes to prosper and flourishe, And discord decayeth and distroyeth the same, And that there can be noe peace where there are noe lawes to relieue and reward the honest and virtuouse, and to corecte and chastize the dissolute and wicked; And whereas our late Soveraigne Lord Kinge James of Blessed Memory, by his highnes letters Patentes, did graunte vnto the Bayliffes and the Cittizens of the said Cittie of Lichfeild, and their Successors for ever (emongst diverse and sundry other Priviledges, liberties, and thinges therein contayned), That the Bayliffes and the One and Twenty Bretheren of the said Cittie for the tyme being, or the maior parte of them, should for ever from thenceforthe haue full power, faculty, and authoritie, at their pleasures, to make, ordayne, constitute and appoynte, Orders, Constitutions, and Ordynances in writinge, vnder the Common Seale of the said Cittie for the good gouveringe, ordering and disposinge of the said Cittie, and of all and singuler the Cittizens, Officers and Ministers,

[margin notes: The 2 Bailiffs and 21 Brethren of the Corporation of Lichfield greet you. 1630. As peace cannot exist unless laws reward the virtuous and chastise the wicked; and as James I. empowered the Bailiffs and Brethren of Lichfield to make Ordinances]

Lichfield Smiths. Second Ordinances, 1630.

<small>for the Trade-Fraternities,</small> Trades and Tradesmen, fraternities, and severall Companies or societies of any Mistery or Occupacion whatsoever within the said Cittie, the liberties and Precinctes of the same, And how and in what manner and forme all and singuler the Cittizens, Artificers, Tradesmen, Fraternities, and all and every the severall Companies of any Trade, Mistery, or occupacion within the said Cittie for the tyme beinge, in their severall Trades, Misteries and occupacions, And how and in what manner euery forreyne Artifecer and Tradesman resortinge to the said Cittie, should vse, gouverne, and behaue him and them selues within the said Cittie, the liberties and precinctes of the same, as by the said letters patentes more fully appeareth : **And whereas** Iohn Mynshawe the now Master, and George Attkyn, and William Smythe the now Wardens, and the Company of Smythes, Goldesmithes, Cardmakers and Ironmongers, Pewterers and Brasyers, Plumbers, Cuttlers, Naylers and Spurryers, within the said Cittie of Lichfeild, beinge a very auncyent society and brotherhood within the said Cittie, perceivinge theire Trades and Craftes to goe to decaye mightely within the said Cittie, as well for want of good order and aduyce emongest them for the better gouverninge and orderinge of the said Trades and Tradesmen, as alsoe for that many Straungers and younge men, which haue not served their apprentishippes within the said Cittie, and many other which haue shifted abroade in the Country, and haue not orderly served any Apprentishipp in any one place, haue hither repayred, and sett vpp the said Trades or some of them, by meanes whereof the freemen of the said Trades within the said Cittie are much hindered and ympoverished, **haue** made humble peticion to vs to graunte them a Booke, for the reforminge and amendinge of the said abuses and inconvenyencies, and for the establishinge of diverse good orders and

<small>and fix how the Tradesmen</small>

<small>and Strangers should behave in Lichfield;</small>

<small>and as the Master and Wardens</small>

<small>of the Smiths, Ironmongers, Cutlers, Spinners, &c. of Lichfield,</small>

<small>seeing that their trades need better ordering,</small>

<small>and that Strangers</small>

<small>not apprentist in the City set up there,</small>

<small>have askt us for fresh</small>

Ordynances emongest them, for the better government of all and every of the said Trades and Brotherhood, and of all persons vsinge the said trades, or any of them, within the said Cittie; **wherevppon**, wee the said Bayliffes, and the One and Twenty Bretheren of the Incorporacion of the said Cittie, with one consent and agreement, takinge into consideracion the cause of the great decay of the said Trades and Tradesmen within the said Cittie, and desiringe to prevent the like inconvenyencies, by ordayninge and appoyntinge some good orders and ordynances for the better government of all and every of the said Trades and Misteries, Haue—accordinge to the power given vnto vs by the said letters Patentes—devised, made, ordayned and appoynted, And by theise presentes doe devise, make, ordayne and appoynte, All and singuler theise orders, constitutions and ordynances followinge, for the good and prosperose estate of all and every of the said Trades and Misteries of Smythes, Goldesmithes, Cardmakers and Ironmongers, Pewterers and Brasyers, Plumbers, Cuttlers, Naylers and Spurryers, within the said Cittie: and for the orderinge, rulinge and governinge of all and every of the Tradesmen of all and every of the said trades within the said Cittie, the liberties and precinctes of the same, Or which shall vse the said Trades or any of them within the liberties of the said Cittie: /

Ordinances for their Trades,

We, the 2 Bailiffs and 21 Brethren of the Corporation of Lichfield,

make and ordain the following Ordinances for the Smiths, Cardmakers, Brasiers, Nailers, &c., in our City:—

1. **Inprimis**, accordinge to the Commendable Custome vsed, as well in the said Cittie as in other Citties and Townes within this Realme of England, That the Gouvernors of Corporacions, Fellowshipps and Societies, are yearly changed, and new chosen in theire places, It is now therefore by vs ordered and ordayned, that yearly and every yeare hereafter, vppon the Wednesday nexte after the feaste daie of St. Clementt, The Maister, Wardens and Com-

1. Every year, on the Wednesday after Nov. 23,

Lichfield Smiths. Second Ordinances, 1630.

<small>the Trades shall meet,</small>

pany, of Smythes, Gouldsmythes, Cardmakers and Ironmongers, Pewterers and Brasyers, Plumbers, Cuttlers, Naylers and Spurryers within the said Cittie, or the Maior parte of them, shall meete together at some place convenyent within the said Cittie; Where the greater nomber of them soe meetinge together, shall

<small>and shall elect a new Master and 2 Wardens</small>

and may proceede to the new election of a new Master and Two new Wardens. And when theire election is soe made, the Master and Wardens soe chosen shall continue respectiuely Master and Wardens of the said

<small>for a year,</small>

Company for one whole yeare then nexte followinge, vntill a new Master and Two new Wardens be chosen

<small>to govern the Company.</small>

as aforesaid, for the ruleinge and government of the said Company, and for the redressinge of all disorders therein, and for the execucion of all Ordynances herein

<small>But if any Officer die or leave the City, &c.,</small>

mencioned. Neverthelesse, yf the said Master and Wardens for the tyme beinge, or any of them, shall die within the yeare, or departe oute of the said Cittie and dwell elswhere, or shall be lawfully putt oute of

<small>the Company</small>

his said Office, Then the Bretheren of the said Company shall in every such case as ocasyon serveth, call

<small>shall meet within 20 days</small>

a new assembly at some convenyent place within the said Cittie, within the space of Twenty daies nexte after such deathe, departure forthe of the said Cittie,

<small>and elect substitutes for the rest of the year.</small>

or puttinge furthe of Office as aforesaid, and proceede to a new election in manner and forme aforesaid, to supply every such defecte, and to continue oute the remnant of the yeare in which such defecte hapneth.

<small>Any Freeman who,</small>

And yf any, beinge a Freeman of any of the said Trades and Misteries within the said Cittie, shall—

<small>after notice,</small>

after notice given or sent vnto him of the tyme and place by the Master and Wardens of the said Trades and Misteries, or by any of them for the tyme beinge—

<small>is absent from an Election without good excuse,</small>

wilfully or without reasonable excuse to be allowed by the Maior parte of the said Company, absent him selfe, and not be present at every such eleccion within the

Lichfield Smiths. Second Ordinances, 1630.

said Cittie, That then every Freeman of the said Trades, or any of them, soe beinge absent, shall forfeyte for every tyme that he shall soe absent him-selfe, vnto the vse of the said Company ij^s vj^d, which said sume shall be putt into theire Common Boxe./ *shall forfeit 2s. 6d.*

2. **Item**, it is further ordayned and ordered, that yf the Master or eyther of the Wardens soe duely elected, shall refuse to take vppon him the said Office or place wherevnto he is elected, or shall (after that he hath taken vppon him the said place) be wilfully negligent in the due execucion of the said Office, or doe neglecte to performe and doe his Office and duety therein, and that he be soe adiudged by the Maior parte of the said Companye vppon examinacion thereof, he shall forfeyte to the vse of the said Company, for every such refusall or wilfull neglecte, Fourtie shillinges; which said summe shall be likewise putt and kepte in theire common Boxe./ *2. [New.] Any Master or Warden refusing the office or neglecting this duty shall forfeit 40s.*

3. **Item**, it is ordayned and further ordered that euery one that hathe, or hereafter shall haue, served his Apprentishipp in or to any of the said Craftes and occupacions within the said Cittie, for the space of Seaven yeares, or for any longer tearme, vnto any freeman of the said Company, shall by his Master be made free onely of the said Mistery and trade which he hath soe served in, and shall be admitted and allowed to be a freeman of the said Company of Smythes, Goldesmythes, Cardmakers and Ironmongers, Pewterers and Brasiers, Plumbers, Cuttlers, Naylers, and Spurryers, yf the said servant doe desire the same, And doe forthwith paie to the Master and Wardens of the said Company for the tyme beinge, for his freedome, Twenty Shillinges; And to the Bayliffes of the said Cittie, or one of them, for the tyme beinge, for swearinge of him a Freeman of the said Cittie and Company, Three shillinges and Foure pence; And to *3. Seven-year Apprentices to any Freeman shall be made free by him of the Company on paying 20s. to it, [new] 3s. 4d. to the City-Bailiffs,*

and 3s. 4d. to the Town-Clerk.	the Towneclarke of the said Cittie for the tyme beinge, for the inrollinge of his name and freedome, Three shillinges and Foure pence; Vppon payne that every person offendinge againste this Ordynance shall forfeyte
Penalty 40s.	to the vse of the said Company, Fourtie shillinges; which said summe shall be likewise putt and kepte in their Common Boxe: /
4. No Brother shall take an Apprentice for less than 7 years.	4. **Item**, it is further ordered and ordayned that noe brother of the said Company shall at any tyme hereafter take any Apprentice vnto any of the said Trades for any shorter tearme then Seaven yeares, Vppon Payne that every Brother of the said Company which shall offend agaynste this Ordynance, shall for- feyte to the vse of the said Company for every tyme
Penalty 40s.	soe offendinge, Fourty shillinges; which said summe shall likewise be putt and kepte in theire Common Boxe./
5. Every Appren- tice when taken	5. **Item**, it is further ordered and ordayned that every Brother of the said Company, which now is or hereafter shall be, which shall take any Apprentice to be instructed in any of the said Trades,
shall be enrold in the Company's Book at its next Meeting,	shall at the nexte meetinge of the said Company, after the retayner of any such Apprentice, procure and cause the name of his Apprentice to be inrolled in a Booke for their [? that] purpose to be appoynted by the Master of the said Company for the tyme beinge, for the inrollinge of the names of all such Apprentices which[1] every freeman of the said Company shall take, and the tyme that he is to serve him therein; Every
[new] his Master paying 12d. to the Master of the Company,	such Brother takinge an Apprentice as aforesaid, pay- inge to the vse onely of the said Master of the said Company for the time beinge, for the inrollinge of the name of his Apprentice in the said Booke, the summe
and 12d. to the Clerk.	of Twelue pence, and to theire Clarke or other Officer, Twelue pence (which said Booke shall from tyme to

[1] *which* for our *as.*

tyme remayne with the Master of the said Company for the tyme beinge), Vppon payne that euery Master of any such servant or Apprentice offendinge agaynste this Ordynance, shall forfeyt for euery Moneth soe offendinge, vnto the vse of the said Company, Tenn shillinges; which shall be likewise putt and kepte in their Common Boxe: / *Penalty 10s.*

6. Item, it is further ordered and ordayned that noe brother of the said Company shall at any tyme hereafter take and keepe aboue one Apprentice at once, nor haue aboue one Apprentice in his service at any tyme together (Excepte it bee in the last yeare wherein his said Apprentice is to serue him), Vppon payne to forfeyte vnto the vse of the said Company, for euery tyme that he shall soe offend, Fiue poundes, which shall be likewise putt and kepte in theire Common Boxe./ *6. No Brother shall have more than one Apprentice at a time.* *Penalty £5.*

7. Item, it is ordered and ordayned that noe Forreyner or stranger of any of the said Trades, or any other person or persons whatsoever, which hath not served Seauen yeares at the leaste as an Apprentice in the said occupacions of Smythes, Goldesmythes, Cardmakers and Ironmongers, Pewterers and Brasyers, Plumbers, Cuttlers, Naylers and Spurryers, or to some of them, to some Brother and Freeman of the said Company, within the said Cittie, shall from henceforth buy, sell, or vtter any kinde of Wares or stuffe [belong]inge or appertayninge to any of the said Trades, within the said Cittie, Excepte only vppon faire daies and Markett daies here, and then betwene the howers hereafter mencioned and appoynted (Savinge that all and every of the Inhabitantes within the said Cittie, which are noe freemen of the said Company may from tyme to tyme, sell within theire dwellinge howses, vnto any person or persons whatsoever, any of theire householde stuffe or ymplementes of howshold, belong- *7. No Stranger or others who haven't servd 7 years' apprenticeship to a Freeman,* *may sell any ware of the Company's trades,* *except on Fairdays and Marketdays.*

GILDS. F

Nor may Strangers buy any silver, gold, jewels,	inge to any of the said Trades); Nor shall any such forreyner buy within the said Cittie, any Wares, Silver or gold, Silver plate, whole or broken, or any manner of preciose stones, or Iewelles, brasse, pewter, lattyn, or
or metal,	lattyn wyer, Mettles or Commodities belonginge to the said Trades of a Goldesmyth, Pewterer and Brasyer, Cardmaker and Ironmonger, or to any of the said
to sell again;	Trades aboue mencioned, to sell the same agayne, or to
nor carry on any of the Company's trades,	make profitt or benifitt thereof; Nor shall sett vpp any Shopp, or vse or exercise any of the said Trades of Smythes, Goldesmythes, Cardmakers and Ironmongers, Pewterers and Brasyers, Plumbers, Cuttlers, Naylers and Spurryers, or any of them, or any thinge to any of the said Trades appertayninge, publiquely or privately,
or be a Freeman of it, until he's compounded with it,	within the said Cittie, or be made a freeman of the said Company, before he hathe compounded for his freedome with the Maior parte of the Freemen of the
or paid it £10,	said Company, or given vnto them the summe of Tenn poundes to be made a Freeman and Brother of the said
and taken his Oath as a Freeman.	Company, and hath taken his oath of a Freeman of the said Cittie and Occupacion accordingly, in such manner & forme as by the precedent Orders is lymited and appoynted for freemen of the said Company to doe; vppon payne that every person that shall doe contrary to any branche or clause of this Ordynance [or] any parte thereof, to forfeyte to the vse of the said Company for every tyme that he shall offend
Penalty 20s.	herein, Twenty shillinges of lawfull money [of] England; which said forfeytures shall be likewise putt and kepte in theire common boxe. And it is alsoe the
No Goldsmith shall meddle with a Pewterer or Brasier, or either of them with him.	true intent and meaning [of] this Ordynance, that the Goldesmyth shall not meddle in the Trade of a Pewterer or Brasyer, nor the Pewterer or Brasier in [the Trade] of a Goldesmyth within the said Cittie: /

Lichfield Smiths. Second Ordinances, 1630.

8.[1] **Item**, it is ordered and ordayned, that noe Iournyman Smyth, Iournyman Goldesmyth, Iournyman Cardmaker and Ironmonger, Iournyman Pewterer and Brasyer, Iournyman Plumber, Iournyman Cuttler, Iournyman Nayler, and Iournyman Spurryer, or any of them, now worckinge, or which at any tyme hereafter shall worcke with any Freeman of the said Company, shall departe from the service of his Master to worcke with any other Brother of this Company, Withoute one Monethes warninge given to his said Master, vnlesse that he haue his Masters license or leaue, Vppon payne that every Brother of the Company which shall receiue any Iournyman contrary to this Ordynance, shall forfeyte to the vse of the said Company for every tyme soe offendinge, Tenn shillinges; Which said Summe shall be likewise putt and kepte in theire Common Boxe: /

8. No Journeyman working for a Freeman shall leave without such Master's license. Penalty 10s.

9. **Item**, it is ordayned and ordered that noe brother of the said Company within the said Cittie, shall from henceforthe suffer any Forreyner or other of any of the said Trades (Excepte such as are his Iournymen and Apprentices) to worcke in his Shopp or howse, or elsewhere within the said Cittie, for him, or for any other person whatsoever, Withoute the licence of the Master or Wardens of the said Company for the tyme beinge; Vppon payne to forfayte for every such offence, to the vse of the said Company, Three shillinges and Fourepence; Which said summe is likewise to be putt and kepte in theire common boxe./

9. No Brother shall employ a Stranger without leave of the Master or Wardens of the Company. Penalty 3s. 4d.

10. **Item**, it is further ordered and ordayned, that yf any Brother of this Company shall refuse to giue or paye, or shall not pay his or theire parte and porcion in money, Which shall be assessed vppon him by the Maior parte of the said Company,

10. [New.] If any Brother doesn't pay his share

[1] 2nd skin of parchment.

Lichfield Smiths. Second Ordinances, 1630.

of the cost of these Ordinances,
he can't make his Apprentices Freemen.

for and towards the obtayninge of theise new Orders and Ordynances, he shall not be hereafter suffered, but shall be for ever disabled, to make any of his Apprentices, which now he hath or hereafter shall haue, Freemen of the said Company, or of any of the said Craftes or occupacions within the said Cittie, at the end of theire Apprentishipps, Any former Order or Ordynance whatsoever to the Contrary thereof notwithstandinge : /

11. No Stranger shall

(save on Fairdays) hawk any goods in which the Company deals.
[See Ordin. 15.]

Penalty 6s. 8d.

11. Item, it is further ordered and ordayned that noe Forreyner exercisinge or vsinge any of the said Trades or Misteries, shall at any tyme on the Markett daies here, or on any other daies (Excepte fayre dayes here) hauke vpp and downe, or in the said Cittie, With any Commodities belonginge to any of the said Trades or Misteries; Vppon payne to forfeyte to the vse of the said Company for every such Offence, the summe of Sixe shillinges and Eighte pence ; Which said summe shall be likewise putt and kepte in theire common Boxe : /

12. No Blacksmith

shall go or send to any inn or house

unless he is orderd ;
nor shall he bribe servants,

to get custom.

Penalty 6s. 8d.

12. Item, it is further ordayned and ordered, that noe brother of the said Company, of the Trade of Blackesmithes within the said Cittie, shall from henceforthe goe to any Innes or howses within the said Cittie, or send any of his servants thither, to doe any thinge belonginge to the said Trade (Excepte he be called or sent for) ; Neyther shall any of them giue rewardes, olde fees or money, to the servantes of any of the said Innes or howses, or to any other person or persons whatsoever, to haue the Custome of the said Inn or howse ; Vppon payne to forfeyte to the vse of the said Company for every such Offence, the summe of Sixe Shillings and Eighte pence : Which said summe shall be likewise putt and kepte in theire Common Boxe.

Lichfield Smiths. Second Ordinances, 1630.

13. **Item**, it is further ordered and ordayned, that no Forreyner vsinge any of the said Craftes or Misteries, shall carry any worcke oute of the said Cittie, belonginge to any of the said Craftes or Misteries, to worcke it vpp in the Country, withoute the consent of the Master and Wardens of the said Company for the tyme beinge; Vppon payne of every one offendinge againste this ordynance, to forfeyte to the vse of the said Company, for every such offence, the summe of Tenn shillinges; Which said summe shall be likewise putt and kepte in theire Common Boxe:/

13. No Stranger shall carry work out of the City to do it in the Country, without leave.

Penalty 10s.

14. **Item**, it is further ordered and ordayned, that noe Iournyman of any of the said Craftes or Misteries, shall at any tyme hereafter, worke within the said Cittie, in his owne howse, or any other Shopp or Roome within the said Cittie (Excepte in a Freemans shopp of the said Company), any thinge appertayninge to any of the said Trades or Misteries, vppon payne to forfeyte to the vse of the said Company, for every tyme wherein he shall offend contrary to this Ordynance, the summe of Three shillinges and Fowre pence; which said summe shall be likewise putt and kepte in theire common boxe:/

14. No Journeyman shall work elsewhere than in a Freeman's shop or room.

Penalty 3s. 4d.

15. **Item**, it is further ordered and ordayned, that noe forreyner vsinge any of the said Craftes, Trades, or Misteries, shall at any tyme hereafter, take any shoppe or standinge, or vtter any Wares within the said Cittie, belonginge to any of the said Craftes or Misteries, but only on the fayre daies, and Markett daies here, videlicet, on the Markett daies here betwixte the howers onely of Tenn of the Clocke in the Morninge, and Three of the Clocke in the Afternoone; Nor shall sell or vtter on the Markett daies here, betwene the said howers, any other kinde of Wares, but onely such Wares as properly belonge vnto

15 (see 11). No Stranger shall take a shop or stand, save on Fair-days, and on Market-days, between 10 a.m. and 3 p.m., or sell any Wares except those of

the Trade wherevnto hee was Apprentice, and truly served his Apprentishipp; Vppon payne to forfeyte for every time offendinge againste this Ordynance, to the vse of the said Company, Fourtie shillinges; Which said summe shall be likewise putt and kepte in theire common boxe.

the trade he was apprentist to.

Penalty 40s.

16. **I**tem, it is further ordered and ordayned, that noe brother of the said Company shall at any tyme hereafter vse and occupy, or cause to be vsed and occupyed, any of the said Craftes or Misteries within the said Cittie, but that wherevnto and wherein he hath served his Apprentishipp; Nor shall sell, or buy to sell agayne, any manner of Wares belonginge to any of the said Craftes or Misteries, but only such Wares as proparrly appertayne to his Trade, whervnto he served his Apprentishipp; vppon payne to forfeyte to the vse of the said Company for every tyme soe offendinge againste this Ordynance, the summe of Tenn shillinges; Which said summe shall be likewise putt and kepte in theire Common Boxe. /

16. No Brother shall

carry on any trade save that he was apprentist to,

or sell any wares save those of such trade.

Penalty 10s.

17. **I**tem, it is further ordered and ordayned, that noe brother of the said Company shall at any tyme hereafter buy, or cause to be boughte, any manner of Wares which any other brother of the said Company hath bargayned, agreed, or given earnest for (yf he haue notice of the same), Vppon payne to forfeyte for every such Offence, to the vse of the said Company, the summe of Tenn shillinges; which shall be likewise put & kept in theire common Boxe : /

17. No Brother shall

buy any Wares that another Brother has bargaind for.

Penalty 10s.

18.[1] **I**tem, it is further ordered and ordayned, that yf any Brothir of the said Company shall happen to die, havinge any Apprentice or Apprentices which at the tyme of his decease haue not served oute hys and theire Apprentishipps, that then the said Apprentice and Apprentices shall, within con-

18. If a Brother die

his Apprentices

[1] Column 2 of 2nd skin.

venyent tyme after request made, be placed with some other Freeman of the said Company, vntill he haue served oute the residue and full tyme of his Apprentishipp (yf he intend to be free of the said Company), or shall serue oute the residue of his tyme with the Widdow of his said deceased Master, At the discrecion of the Master and Wardens of the said Company for the tyme beinge, or the Maior *parte* of them; or else agree with the Master and Wardens of the said Company for the tyme beinge, for the residue of the tyme he hath to serue, to the vse of his said late Masters widdowe, And soe de*parte* withoute his[1] freedome of the said Company, yf he be soe disposed; vppon payne to forfeyte to the vse of the said Company, for every Offence againste this Ordynance, Fiue poundes, to be likewise putt and kepte in theire com*m*on Boxe.

shall be put with another Freeman,

or remain with their old Master's widow,

or pay dues to her, and leave without their Freedom.

Penalty £5.

19. Item, it is further ordered and ordayned, that the olde Master and Wardens of the said Company shall, every yeare—vppon the daye that the new Master and Wardens of the said Company are chosen—accordinge to the trew meaninge of the former ordynance, make and deliver vpp vnto the new Master and Wardens, and to the rest of the said Company (beinge there p*re*sent) a trew accompte in writinge vnder theire handes, of all such sum*m*es of money, writinges and other thinges whatsoever, Which they or any of them haue received or disbursed for the yeare last p*re*cedinge, by reason of theire Offices of M*a*ster and Wardenshippes; And shall then paye and deliver to the handes of the new Master and Wardens, all arrearages which shall appeare to be due vppon theire accomptes; and vppon payment thereof, the said new Master and Wardens soe chosen, and eyther of them, shall enter into bond, and become bounden ioyntly or severally, with good and sufficyent suerties, in double

19. Every year's Officers shall,

on the election of new Officers,

account to them for all Company-money, &c.,

and pay them all arrears.

The new Officers shall then give Bonds

---

[1] MS. alterd. ? *the* or *his*.

Lichfield Smiths. Second Ordinances, 1630.

to the old one

to account duly at the end of their year.

Penalty £10.

the summe of the money received, to the olde Master and Wardens, or to some other Brother of the said Company whom the maior parte of the said Company shall for that purpose nominate, with condicion to deliver vpp the like accoumpte as aforesaid; vppon payne for every person offendinge againste this Ordynance, for euery such offence to forfeite to the vse of the said Company Tenn poundes; which said summe shall be likewise putt and kepte in theire common Boxe. /

20. All trade-disputes between Freemen shall

be referd to the Master and Wardens,

under a

Penalty of 3s. 4d.

But if they don't arbitrate in 14 days,

the complainer may take his own course.

20. Item, it is ordered and ordayned, that yf any debate, discention or discord, shall happen betwene any of the Freemen of the said Company within the same Cittie, concerninge matters of theire Trade, that the partie grieved shall declare his griefe to the Master and Wardens of the said Company for the tyme beinge, before he seeke any further remedy by lawe; to the intent that every such debate happninge may be friendly ended by the said Master, Wardens and Company; Vppon payne of every one that shall offend herein, or shall refuse to stand to the end that the said Master, Wardens and Company, or the maior parte of them, shall make, to forfeyte for every tyme soe offendinge, to the vse of the said Company, Three shillinges and Foure pence; which summe is likewise to be putt and kepte in theire common Boxe; **Provided** alwaise, that yf the Master, Wardens and Companie, or the maior parte of them for the tyme beinge, doe not end and arbitrate the same within a fortnight nexte after complaynte made vnto them, That then the partie grieved shall be at liberty to take his remedy as he shall thinke beste.

21. All Brethren shall obey the Master and Wardens,

21. Item, it is further ordered and ordayned, that the Master and Wardens of the said Company for the tyme beinge shall be obeyed in all reasonable and lawfull thinges for the tyme of theire Office, by all and every of the Bretheren of the said

Company; And that every person of the said Company shall duely and respectiuely carry and behaue him selfe to the said Master and Wardens and every of them (for the tyme beinge), withoute givinge them or any of them any evill or vnseemely wordes or mysbehaviour; vppon payne that every one that shall doe any thinge contrary to this ordynance, to forfeyte to the vse of the said Company, Three shillinges and Foure pence; which shall be likewise putt and kepte in theire common Boxe. *be respectful to them, and not abuse them. Penalty 3s. 4d.*

22. Item, it is further ordered and ordayned, that noe brother of the said Company shall disclose hereafter any Counsell or Communicacion concerninge the said Trades or Mysteries or any of them, had at theire common assemblies; neyther make any brawles, chidinges or contencions there, nor raise or reporte any false, slaunderose or evill speeches, or tale of any Freeman of the said Company within the said Cittie, vppon payne to forfeyte to the vse of the said Company, for every tyme that any Brother shall offend herein, Tenn shillinges; which summe is likewise to be putt and kepte in theire common Boxe. / *22. No Brother shall disclose Trade secrets, or brawl, or slander any Freeman. Penalty 10s.*

23. Item, it is further ordered and ordayned, that yf any Freeman of the said Craftes or occupacions within the said Cittie, or any forreyner or other person, shall offend in any thinge, againste any of the Ordynances in theise presentes contayned, he shall paye the severall penalties and forfeytures herein mencioned and contayned, to the Master and Wardens of the said Company for the tyme beinge, vppon request made vnto the offendors by the said Master or Wardens for the tyme beinge, or by any of them. And yf any Offendor againste any of theise Ordynances shall not forthwith, vppon request as aforesaid, paie vnto the Master & Wardens of the said Company, or to some of them, the severall penalties which he hath forfeyted, or *23. Offending Freemen shall pay their penalties. If they don't,*

shall forfeyte in or by any of theise Ordynances, Then and from thenceforthe it shall and may be lawfull to and for the Master and Wardens of the said Company for the tyme beinge, or for any of them, to distrayne and take by way of distresse, any of the Goods, Wares and Marchandize of the said Offendors, and the same to detayne and keepe by the space of Three daies then next after; and yf the said Forfeyture or forfeytures for which the said distresse shall happen to be taken, be not within the said Three daies paid and dischardged, That then and from thenceforthe the Master and Wardens of the said Company for the tyme beinge, shall sell the same goods, Wares and Merchandizes, after the best rate they can, for the payment of the penaltie forfeyted; and the overplus comeinge of the sale thereof (yf any be) the same shall be agayne restored vnto the party soe offendinge (he demaundinge the same). And yf it happen that the said Master and Wardens of the said Company for the tyme beinge can not convenyently distrayne the goods of any such Offendor in forme aforesaid, That then in defecte of such distresse, it shall be lawfull to and for the Master and Wardens of the said Company, by the name of the Master and Wardens of the society and Company of Smythes, Goldesmythes, Cardmakers and Ironmongers, Pewterers and Brasyers, Plumbers, Cuttlers, Naylers and Spurryers within the said Cittie, to arrest, sue or ymplead, or cause to be arested, sued and ympleaded, any of the said Offendors by Process yssuing oute of the Kings Maiesties Courts of Record within this Cittie, vppon an action of Dete for any of the said Forfeytures herein contayned, at theire discrecion, o[r for]the of any other of his Maiesties Courtes of Record whatsoever. /

24. Item, it is lastly ordered and ordayned that the said Master, Wardens and Company, shall for ever haue a Common Boxe, Wherein all theire said

severall forfeytures shall be kepte as aforesaid; Which said Boxe shall alwaise from tyme to tyme remayne in the Custody of the Master of the said Company for the tyme beinge; and the moneyes in the said Boxe beinge shall alwaise from tyme to tyme be bestowed and laid forthe, as by the Master, Wardens and Company, or the greater parte of them for the tyme beinge, shalbe appoynted and declared. **Provided** alwayse, and it is hereby further ordered and ordayned, that this Booke,[1] nor any thinge herein contayned, shall extend or be in any sorte preiudiciall to any former Booke or Bookes, orders or ordynances, heretofore made by vs vnto any other Brotherhood or society within this Cittie; But that all and every of the Booke and Bookes heretofore made by vs to them, or any of them, may continue in theire full power and force, accordinge to all and every of the Orders and Ordynances therein respectiuely contayned, Anythinge herein contayned to the contrary thereof in any wise notwithstandinge. **Provided** likewise that yf it shall happen at any tyme hereafter, That there shall not be one sufficyent freeman resident within the said Cittie, of every of the said Trades vsinge his trade and mistery here, That then yf the Master and Wardens of the said Company doe not provide one sufficyent workman of every of the said Trades, to vse and practise his trade here, within Six Moneths next after warninge given vnto them by the Bayliffes of the said Cittie for the tyme beinge, That then and from thenceforth it shall and may be lawfull to and for the Bayliffs and Bretheren of this Incorporacion, to make free of the said Company, at theire liberty and pleasure, any Forreyner of any of the said Trades, which shall be soe wantinge within the said Cittie, Theise Ordynances, or anythinge herein contayned, to the contrary thereof in any wise notwithstandinge. **In witnes whereof,**

to be kept by the Master,

the money in it being laid out by the Officers and Freemen.

Proviso 1: these Ordinances shall not prejudice any other Lichfield Society;

Proviso 2: if hereafter not 1 Freeman of any Company-trade is in Lichfield,

the City Corporation may make any Stranger of that Trade free of the Company.

---

[1] Deed, set of Ordinances.

Seald with the Common Seal of Lichfield, 4 July, 1630.

wee the aforesaid Bayliffes and Bretheren of this Incorporacion, for the better authority of all and every of the aforesaid Ordynances, haue herevnto putt the Common Seale of the aforesaid Citty, the Twentie Fourthe daye of Iuly 1630, And in the Sixte yeare of the Raigne of our Soveraigne Lord, Charles, by the grace of God, of England, Scotland, Fraunce and Ireland, Kinge, defendor of the faithe, &c^t:

[*There is no seal to the Deed.*]

[Endorst in a later hand.] Blacksmiths Company
24 Iuly 1630

Iohn Thornton

[A Third set of Ordinances was engrost for execution, in July 1820, 1 Geo. IV, by Sir Wm. Draper Best, Knight, one of the Judges of the King's Bench, and Sir Jn. Richardson, Knight, one of the Judges of the Common Pleas, but does not seem to have been executed. It has 23 Clauses founded almost wholly on the foregoing Ordinances. I don't think it worth printing.]

ORDINANCES OF THE LYNN TAILORS.

[A.D. 1449.]

From the 11th Report of the Historical MSS. Commission, Appendix, Part III. (1887) p. 165-6, by Mr. J. Cordy Jeafferson.

6 July, 27 Henry VI.—Ordinance by the Mayor and council, made for the good government of the Craft of taillours of the toun of Bishop's Lenn, wherby it was appointed that yearly all tailors, plying their craft in the said toun should appear before the Mayor in the Guildhall within the two months following St. Michael's Feast, and in his presence choose two of their number to act as Hedesmen of their craft during the ensuing twelve months; who on their election should (p. 166) take the following oath :—

"Sires, ye shal wele duly and trewely make serche of your crafte of all dwellers within the toun att this time; and that from this tyme forward, no new-come persones sette uppe the saide crafte with-oute he be sufficiaunt in connyng, Whos sufficiaunce and connyng shal be determined bi þe advyse of the meyre and the said hedesmen. And every persone so newe come and omitted, and wilbe no burgeys, for his newe settyng uppe shal paye to the Meyre xld., to the comons of Lenn xld., and to the said hedesmen xld.—Which xld. shal go to the sustentacioun of the procession upon Corpus Christi day ;—And yf he wil be burgeys, than he to pay but xld. for his no [? so] newe settyng uppe;

Henceforth no Tailor shall set up unless he have skill, in the judgment of the Mayor and Headsmen.

Any who won't be a Burgess, is to pay 3 sums of 40d. each;

Any who will be a Burgess, only one 40d.

Ordinances of the Lynn Tailors.

All to pay for every Denizen sower ¼d a week;

and for every alien, double.

[And also to pay] to þe said hedesmen, for every sower be the weke, denysen *quadranta* [¼d] ; for every sower be the quarter, denysen iid. ; and for every sower of alyaunt, duble to þe sower of deynsens, upon the payne the seid dwellers paye duble hem selffe. And

A non-Burgess to pay 40d. for every apprentice.

also, what persone of the saide crafte kepe any prentys with-in the toun from this tyme forward, and be no burgeys, shal paye to þe sustentacioun of the seid procession on Corpus Christi day xld. ; and the Meyre to sette a rewele therein, according to þe statute in the

Any one misfitting a customer, or cabbaging his cloth,

Hall of olde tyme. And yf any persone compleyne of any man of the seid crafte þat he hath hurte be mysse-cuttyng or mysse-shapyng, or any part of his clothe taken otherwyse than in trewe forme ; upon which, any persone or persones so convicted be leful and due preves, þat þan he or they so convycted, to

shall make amends.

make amendes to þe party or partyes so greved, be the sight of the Meyre and the seid hedesmen. And yf

But a Tailor unjustifiably slandering another on this point,

any persone of the said crafte slandre any man of such deedis so doon, and may not evydently be preved be due and leeful preves, they to be punysshed be þe avyse of

is to forfeit 40d.

þe Meyre and the seid hedesmen, and to forfite as often as he is founden so fauty, xld., Which shull go to þe

Non-tailors slandering, are to be punished.

seid procession upon Corpus Christi day. And yf any other person than of the said crafte compleyn or slaundre any man of dedis so doon, and may not be duly preved, thei to be punysshed be advyse of the Meyre and his

All quarrels in the Trade to be referred to the 2 Headsmen, and

counsell. And yf ther be any controversies and debates among any of the seid crafte—shaper or sower,—noon of them to sewe other in no manere wyse, but to come to the ii hedesmen, and to compleyne to him yf nede be ; and thei to do .ther parte to drawe hem to accorde ; and

then the Mayor,

yf thei may not, þat þan thei to make relacion to Meyre :

under a fixt penalty.

every man doying the contrary shal [forfete] þe payne

And if a Headsman is partial

accordyng to þe statute in the halle. and yf any of the seid ii hedesmen wil be parciall, or rewle þe mater otherwise þan conciens, that than he þat so feleþ him agreved, come and compleyne to the Meyre. And if any þe said hedesmen be slowe [slow], and wil not do as is aforenseid, so that they departe without remedy, so that who of hem sewe other throwe here defaute, that iche of þe seid hedesmen so preved gilty, to forfete þe peyne þat longeth to the halle," etc. [Followed by the names of the thirty-eight tailors of Lynn affected by the statute.] or dilatory,

he shall pay the regular penalty.

SOUTHAMPTON TAILORS' PETITIONS.

[A.D. 1406-7 and 1468.]

11th Report of the Historical MSS. Commission (1877), Appendix III. p. 11, by Mr. J. Cordy Jeafferson.

8 Henry IV.—Petition (French) of the Taylors of Southampton to the Mayor, Aldermen, and Burgesses of the said town, together with record of consent of the same Mayor, Aldermen and burgesses to the same petition, which, in the clauses following the preamble, runs in the following words:—

"Please a votre tressage discrecion, par advys de voz Aldermans, prudeshommes, et autres voz avaunditz bones burgeis, ordeigner et establler en icest present assemblee, que nulle aliene Tailloure, ne soudier Taillour Engleis, ne autre veignant en Carrike, Galeye, ou nief des aliens, priegne ne tiegne shope, meson, ne chambre, deinz mesme la ville pour tailler, ne deinz la Fraunchise dicelle taille robes, jepone, ne autres garnementz, a qi que soient, devaunt que tielle Taillour aliene ou soudier Taillour ad fait fyn et gree ove les mestres de mesme de mestier pour le temps esteauntz, sur peyne denprisonement, et ceo le primer foitz que soit trove trespassaunt encountre ceste ordynaunce; et le secunde foitz dencorger la peyne de C.s. a leuer par le

Pray ordain that no alien, or hired English tailor, or other from an alien shop, may set up in the city to cut

or may cut robes, &c.,

till he has settled with the Masters of the Trade, on

pain of imprisonment the first time

and 100s. the 2nd time;

And that no strange tailor may take shop or room till he has leave of the Mayor and Masters and has paid dues.

commaundement de vous ou del mair pour le temps esteauntz, par les ministres de dite ville . . . Et auxi que nulle Taillour estraunge veignant sodeynement de tailler en mesme la ville, ne tiegne shope ne chambre de tailler drape, saunz conge del Maire et des mestres del dit mestier, et tanque il ad feat fyn solons lour discreciouns en manere suis dit. Et, &c. &c."

Ibid. p. 87. A.D. 1468 : 12 December, 8 Edward IV.

Certificatory Letters, touching the petition made to the Mayor, bailiffs and burgesses of Southampton by the Tailors of the said town, and the consent of the same Mayor, &c. to the said petition, whereby the tailors of Southampton sought for the protection of their trade against the encroachments and competition of foreign tailors.

After stating that heretofore their gains have been "wonte to rise of the strange people comynge into the poorte of the saied towne, as in carryckes, galleys, shippes of Spayne, Portingall, Almayne, Flanders, Zelonde, and others, in their vyages, ther beynge for their use to cutte their clothe by the handes of the taylors of the same town," John Renande (Roeffe Taylor) and the petitioners of the Craft of Tailors of Southampton complain that, to their injury "Nowe of late in dyvers carrickes, galleys, and in shippes of strangers, have come taylers of divers nacions, and sondre in them by divers tymes, the which tary and abyde within the carrickes, galleyes and shippes within the same poorte," &c.

See extracts about the crafts of webbers and weavers, and shoemakers and cordaners of Waterford in the 10th Report, Appendix, Pt. VI. p. 319, 320, and many other trade regulations. Very interesting details about the Galway trades, &c. are in the same Report : Appendix, Part VI. Notes of Ordinances for plenty of trades in

Kendal are in the 10th Report: Appendix, Part IV. p. 299-318. That about the Tailors is as follows:

f. 221.—" Orders concerninge Tailors." February 23, 1575. It is ordered that the Company of Tailors may nominate four of the most honest members of their trade, to be called Searchers or Overseers, to correct abuses. (This order was repealed in March 1575.) It is also ordered that no person who has not given or promised a benevolence or gift towards purchasing the incorporation of the borough, and so become a freeman, or been made free after, shall take upon him the occupation of a tailor within the borough, under pain to forfeit 10s. to the chamber of the borough. It is also ordered that any tailor may at pleasure exercise the science of a woollen draper. (The last two orders having been repealed, were revived on the 14th of November 1577.) . . . . .

f. 231. List of the twelve Companies [? 1578] with the number of wardens eligible by each :—

1. Chapmen, Merchants and Salters, 2.
2. Mercers and Drapers, linen and woollen, 2.
3. Shearmen, Fullers, Dyers, and Websters, 4.
4. Tailors, Embroiderers and Whilters, 4 or 2.
5. Cordwainers (cordyners), Cobblers, and Curriers, 4 or 2.
6. Tanners, Saddlers, and Girdlers, 2.
7. Inn-holders, Alehouse-keepers, and Tiplers, 4.
8. Butchers and Fishers, 2.
9. Cardmakers and Wiredrawers, 2.
10. Surgeons, Scriveners, Barbers, Glovers, Skinners, Parchment and Point-makers, 2.
11. Smiths, Iron and Hardware-men, Armourers, Cutlers, Bowyers, Fletchers, Spurriers, Potters, Painters, Plumbers, Tinkers, Pewterers, and Metallers, 2.
12. Carpenters, Joiners, Masons, Wallers, Slaters, Thatchers, Glaziers, Painters, Plasterers, Daubers, Pavers, Millers, and Coopers, 2.

Notes are in the Ninth Report, p. 292a, of the Stratford-on-Avon Ordinances for Weavers (2 April, 14 Eliz., A.D. 1572), Shoemakers and Sadlers (21 Oct., 20 Eliz., A.D. 1578), and Skinners and Tailors (2 March, 1585).

For notes of other Ordinances, and of many Gilds—chiefly religious—I refer the student to these Hist. MSS. Com. Reports, which contain material for a most interesting volume of extracts on the social condition of the country. I hope Mr. W. L. Sydney will some day give us such a volume, to match the capital " England in the Eighteenth Century."

The manufacturer's authorised representative in the EU for product safety is Oxford University Press España S.A. of El Parque Empresarial San Fernando de Henares, Avenida de Castilla, 2 - 28830 Madrid (www.oup.es/en or product.safety@oup.com). OUP España S.A. also acts as importer into Spain of products made by the manufacturer.
Printed and bound by CPI Group (UK) Ltd, Croydon, CR0 4YY

20/03/2026

02075339-0005